Earth Science Success: 50 Lesson Plans for Grades 6-9

Earth Science Success: 50 Lesson Plans for Grades 6–9

by Catherine Oates-Bockenstedt and Michael Oates

"The art of teaching is the art of assisting discovery."

Mark Van Doren (1894–1972)

NSTA press

National Science Teachers Association

Arlington, Virginia

Claire Reinburg, Director
Jennifer Horak, Managing Editor
Judy Cusick, Senior Editor
Andrew Cocke, Associate Editor
Betty Smith, Associate Editor

ART AND DESIGN
Will Thomas Jr., Art Director
Cover Illustration - Tyson Mangelsdorf

PRINTING AND PRODUCTION
Catherine Lorrain, Director
Nguyet Tran, Assistant Production Manager

National Science Teachers Association
Francis Q. Eberle, Executive Director
David Beacom, Publisher

Library of Congress Cataloging-in-Publication Data

Oates-Bockenstedt, Catherine.
  Earth science success: 50 lesson plans for grades 6-9 / by Catherine Oates-Bockenstedt and Michael D. Oates.
       p. cm.
  Includes bibliographical references and index.
  ISBN 978-1-933531-35-9
1. Earth sciences—Study and teaching (Middle school)—United States.
2. Lesson planning—United States. I. Oates, Michael. II. Title.
  QE47.A1O28 2008
  372.35—dc22
          2008025058

NSTA is committed to publishing material that promotes the best in inquiry-based science education. However, conditions of actual use may vary and the safety procedures and practices described in this book are intended to serve only as a guide. Additional precautionary measures may be required. NSTA and the author(s)s do not warrant or represent that the procedures and practices in this book meet any safety code or standard of federal, state, or local regulations. NSTA and the author(s) disclaim any liability for personal injury or damage to property arising out of or relating to the use of this book, including any of the recommendations, instructions, or materials contained therein.

 Featuring sciLINKS®—a way of connecting text and the Internet. Up-to-the-minute online content, classroom ideas, and other materials are just a click away.

Contents

Contents

Introduction

Preface

Earth Science Success: 50 Lesson Plans for Grades 6–9 is a one-year Earth science curriculum with clear day-by-day lessons in the areas of astronomy, geology, meteorology, and physical oceanography. Intended for teachers of grades 6–9, *Earth Science Success* emphasizes hands-on, sequential experiences through which students discover important science concepts lab by lab and develop critical thinking skills. The 50 lesson plans mentioned in the title include 33 investigations (labs), found in the chapters of this book, and 17 detailed projects (pretest, science activities, etc.), found in Appendix B.

The National Assessment of Educational Progress (NAEP), from the U.S. Department of Education, evaluates both basic skills and critical thinking skills in education (Campbell, Hombo, and Mazzeo 2000). NAEP has found that emphasizing hands-on activities that allow students to explore theory results in meaningful science learning. In addition, NAEP has established that traditional activities—teaching the facts of science by completing worksheets and reading primarily from textbooks—have no positive effects on science learning. The Trends in International Mathematics and Science Study (TIMSS) provides further evidence of the benefits of hands-on teaching for meaning (Stigler and Hiebert 1999). By the time students reach middle school, using hands-on activities to teach meaning in science becomes critical. Increased motivation and higher levels of academic engagement are both benefits, and prerequisites, for academic success in middle school.

The topics chosen and the laboratory approach employed in *Earth Science Success* reflect *National Science Education Standards* (NRC 1996) and both *Atlas of Science Literacy* and *Science for All Americans* (AAAS 2007; 1989). Each lesson builds the scaffolding for the next, in order to promote a solid grasp of the material. Students are actively involved in a process of reflection, investigation, and concept acquisition from the start. All learners construct their own knowledge and understandings from their experiences. The academic knowledge development presented in this book is incremental. Investigations carefully sequenced and connected to previous experiences in order to enable students to successfully build their knowledge. You will find the applicable cross-references for the National Science Education Standards and Benchmarks for Science Literacy in tables at the end of this introduction.

Introduction _____

During the development and field-testing of *Earth Science Success*, care was taken to produce a curriculum that would complement well-known Earth Science print materials through a research-proven investigation methodology. Among the works consulted, three held the greatest influence: the National Science Teachers Association four-volume series Project Earth Science (Ford and Smith 2000); the two-volume J. Weston Walch Hands-on Science series (Fried and McDonnell 2000); and the University of Hawaii Curriculum Research and Development Group series (Pottenger and Young 1992). Each of these would constitute a valuable resource for teachers who have chosen the lab-centered activities of *Earth Science Success* as their main source of lesson plans and student handouts. Along with ideas suggested during field-testing by colleagues, we are also indebted to the National Aeronautics and Space Administration. Two summers spent at NASA's Space Academy for Educators were instrumental in the decision to write this book.

References

American Association for the Advancement of Science (AAAS). 2007. *Atlas of science literacy.* 2 vols. Washington, DC: AAAS.

American Association for the Advancement of Science (AAAS). 1999. *Science for all Americans.* New York: Oxford University Press.

Campbell, J. R., C. M. Hombo, and J. Mazzeo. 2000. *NAEP 1999: Trends in academic progress, Three decades of student performance.* Washington, DC: U.S. Government Printing Office.

Ford, B. A. 2001. *Project earth science: Geology.* Arlington, VA: NSTA Press.

Ford, B. A., and P. S. Smith. 2000. *Project earth science: Physical oceanography.* Arlington, VA: NSTA Press.

Fried, B., and M. McDonnell. 2000. *Walch hands-on science series: Rocks and minerals.* Portland, ME: J. Weston Walch.

Fried, B., and M. McDonnell. 2000. *Walch hands-on science series: Our solar system.* Portland, ME: J. Weston Walch.

National Research Council (NRC). 1996. *National science education standards.* Washington, DC: National Academy Press.

Pottenger, F. M., and D. B. Young. 1992. *The local environment: FAST 1, foundational approaches to science teaching.* Honolulu: University of Hawaii Curriculum Research and Development Group.

Smith, P. S. 2001. *Project earth science:* Astronomy. Arlington, VA: NSTA Press.

Smith, P. S., and B. A. Ford. 2001. *Project earth science: Meteorology.* Arlington, VA: NSTA Press.

Stigler, J. W., and J. Hiebert. 1999. *The teaching gap: Best ideas from the world's teachers for improving education in the classroom.* New York: Free Press

Introduction

To the Earth Science Teacher

The principal author of this book is a middle school Earth Science teacher. Like you, her day is very busy with large classes, meetings and other duties, grading and correction, class preparation, answering e-mail from parents, etc. She is therefore, like you, very much in the trenches with all that the hectic life of a middle school science teacher entails. *Earth Science Success* is the result of her desire to create a ready-to-use, lab-focused, survival-guide curriculum that has been field-tested and refined at Central Middle School in Eden Prairie, Minnesota. Catherine obtained National Board for Professional Teaching Standards Certification (Early Adolescent Science, 2004) while teaching these lessons. Together with her father, an experienced writer and teacher-trainer, she has organized this curriculum into a series of investigations that emphasize the active involvement of students in a discovery process. It is the authors' hope that you will find this book a useful tool as you plan and teach your Earth science classes.

Supplementary activities. Appendix B contains a number of specific activities that will help you to vary your lesson strategies, providing new choices for classroom interactions. Each of these is explained in the appendix and several of them are included in "The First Ten Days" lesson plans found in Chapter 1.

Earth Science Success **on the web.** The National Science Teachers Association website has a link to *Earth Science Success* resources. This contains an electronic version of the student handouts (part 3 of each lab) that should facilitate personalization and reproduction.

We believe that the hands-on approach to Earth science used in this book will help your students relate what they are discovering and learning to their own worlds of experience. Similarly, student misconceptions are more readily identified and dispelled when students are required, in a trusting classroom atmosphere, to reflect on what they know and to share initial hypotheses that they are encouraged to formulate.

Correlations With National Science Education Standards and Benchmarks for Science Literacy

The following tables cross-reference the 33 labs featured in this book with the National Science Education Standards and Benchmarks for Science Literacy. Supplementary projects and activities (see Appendices B and C), while not listed in the table below, meet most of the Standards, as well.

National Science Education Standards	Lab Reference from *Earth Science Success*
A. Science as Inquiry	
(1) Identify Questions That Can Be Answered Through Scientific Investigations	All 33 labs
(2) Design and Conduct a Scientific Investigation	Extension and further investigation sections of all labs, S-1, A-5, G-5, G-7, M-8, O-6, O-7, and O-8.
(3) Use Appropriate Tools and Techniques to Gather, Analyze, and Interpret Data	All 33 labs
(4) Develop Descriptions, Explanations, Predictions, and Models Using Evidence	All 33 labs
(5) Think Critically and Logically to Make the Relationships Between Evidence and Explanations	All 33 labs
(6) Recognize and Analyze Alternative Explanations and Predictions	All 33 labs
(7) Communicate Scientific Procedures and Explanations	All 33 labs
(8) Use Mathematics in Areas of Scientific Inquiry	S-1, A-1, A-2, A-3, A-4, A-5, G-1, G-2, G-4, G-5, M-3, M-4, M-8, O-3, O-4, O-5, O-6, and O-7.

B. Physical Science	
(1) Properties and Changes of Properties in Matter	S-1, G-1, G-2, G-3, M-1, M-2, M-3, M-4, M-5, M-6, O-1, O-2, O-3, and O-7.
(2) Motions and Forces	S-1, A-1, A-2, A-3, A-4, A-5, A-6, A-7, A-8, G-4, G-7, G-8, M-2, M-3, M-5, M-8, O-2, O-3, O-4, O-5, O-6, O-7, and O-8.
(3) Transfer of Energy	A-5, A-8, G-7, G-8, M-3, M-5, M-8, O-3, and O-8.
D. Earth and Space Science	
(1) Structure of the Earth System	A-1, A-2, A-3, A-4, A-5, A-6, A-7, A-8, G-1, G-2, G-3, G-4, G-5, G-6, G-7, G-8, M-1, M-3, M-5, M-8, O-1, O-2, and O-3.
(2) Earth's History	G-4, G-5, M-1, O-2, and O-3.
(3) Earth in the Solar System	A-1, A-2, A-3, A-4, A-5, A-6, A-7, A-8, G-4, M-1, O-1, and O-3.
E. Science and Technology	
(1) Abilities of Technological Design	A-3, A-6, A-8, G-5, M-3, M-7, M-8, O-5, and O-8.
(2) Understandings About Science and Technology	A-6, A-8, G-5, M-7, M-8, O-3, and O-8.
F. Science in Personal and Social Perspectives	
(1) Natural Hazards	G-7, G-8, M-1, M-8, and O-2.
(2) Risks and Benefits	A-6, A-8, G-7, G-8, M-8, O-4, O-5, and O-6.
(3) Science and Technology in Society	A-8, G-5, G-7, G-8, M-4, M-7, M-8, O-3, and O-8.
G. History and Nature of Science	
(1) Science as a Human Endeavor	All 33 labs
(2) Nature of Science	All 33 labs
(3) History of Science	A-4, A-8, G-2, G-4, M-1, M-7, and O-3.

Benchmarks for Science Literacy	Lab Reference from *Earth Science Success*
(1) The Nature of Science	
A. The Scientific World View	All 33 labs
B. Scientific Inquiry	Extension and further investigation sections of all labs, S-1, A-3, A-5, A-6, G-1, G-4, G-5, G-7, M-4, M-8, O-6, O-7, and O-8.
C. The Scientific Enterprise	S-1, A-6, A-8, G-5, G-7, M-7, M-8, and O-3.
(2) The Nature of Mathematics	
A. Patterns and Relationships	A-1, A-2, A-3, A-4, A-5, G-1, G-4, G-5, G-7, M-3, M-4, M-8, O-4, O-5, O-6, and O-7.
B. Mathematics, Science, and Technology	A-1, A-2, A-3, A-4, A-5, A-6, A-7, A-8, G-1, G-4, G-5, G-7, M-4, M-8, O-3, O-4, O-5, O-6, O-7, and O-8.
C. Mathematical Inquiry	Extension and further investigation sections of all labs, A-1, A-2, A-3, A-4, A-5, G-1, G-4, G-5, G-7, M-4, M-8, O-6, and O-7.
(3) The Nature of Technology	
A. Technology and Science	A-3, A-5, A-6, A-8, G-5, G-7, M-4, M-8, O-3, O-6, O-7, and O-8.
(4) The Physical Setting	
A. The Universe	A-1, A-2, A-3, A-4, A-5, A-6, A-7, A-8, G-4, M-1, and O-3.
B. The Earth	A-1, A-2, A-3, A-4, A-5, G-1, G-2, G-3, G-4, G-5, G-6, G-7, G-8, O-1, O-2, and O-3.
C. Processes That Shape the Earth	G-1, G-2, G-3, G-4, G-5, G-6, G-7, G-8, M-1, M-2, O-1, O-2, and O-3.
D. Structure of Matter	S-1, A-4, A-5, G-1, G-2, G-3, M-1, M-3, O-1, O-2, and O-7.

E. Energy Transformations	A-5, A-8, G-7, G-8, M-1, M-2, M-3, M-5, M-7, M-8, O-3, and O-8.
F. Motion	S-1, A-6, A-8, G-7, G-8, M-2, M-3, M-8, O-2, O-3, O-4, O-5, O-6, O-7, and O-8.
G. Forces of Nature	A-1, A-2, A-4, A-5, G-7, G-8, M-1, M-2, M-8, O-1, O-2, and O-3.
(5) The Living Environment	
E. Flow of Matter and Energy	G-3, M-1, and O-3.
(7) Human Society	
A. Cultural Effects on Behavior	S-1, A-6, A-8, G-4, G-5, G-7, G-8, M-1, M-4, M-8, and O-3.
C. Social Change	A-8, G-5, G-7, G-8, M-8, and O-2.
D. Social Trade-Offs	A-3, A-5, A-6, A-8, G-5, G-7, G-8, M-1, M-8, O-4, O-5, O-6, and O-7.

Chapter 1

The Organization of Each Investigation

Chapter 1

Each of the labs in this book is organized to follow a pattern of active involvement by students in the discovery process. These labs include investigations specific to astronomy, geology, meteorology, and physical oceanography, as well as an initial investigation, Lab S-1, which helps introduce students to the fundamental nature of scientific inquiry. In each case, students are continually presented with a three-section process. The three sections are anticipation, data collection, and analysis.

Table 1.1. Anticipation, Data Collection, Analysis

Section	Steps	Purpose
Anticipation	Title and statement of the problem	Initial reflection
	Prediction	Recall of prior knowledge, including misconceptions
	Thinking about the problem	Defining of concepts
Data collection	Materials Procedures Data collection table(s)	Focused student lab work, hands-on collection of data, and opportunities for the formation of a new equilibrium of understanding
Analysis	Summary questions and concluding-the-analysis statements	Reporting of results; follow-up
	Expansion and further investigation	Opportunities for differentiation

Anticipation involves reflection on an anticipatory question, recall of previous knowledge about the topic, discussion of misconceptions, and definition of concepts. *Data collection* is where the hands-on laboratory investigation takes place. *Analysis* requires confirmation or rejection of results, reporting the results, and concluding-the-analysis statements. In addition, once each lab is completed and results have been reported, there are suggestions for enrichment and further investigation. A detailed Science Experiment Project (pp. 1 286–296), as well as various other science projects (e.g., "Edible Stalactites and Stalagmites," "Weather Instrument", "Sink a Sub"), per CMS is also included. Consequently, students are given a broad range of inquiry-related differentiation opportunities.

To facilitate planning and teaching, each investigation (lab) is divided into three parts (Table 1.2). The first part, called the "Teacher's Lesson Plan Outline," offers an overview and notes for the entire lab. The second part, called "Student Lab Notebook Entries," details the portions of the lab report that will be recorded by students in their lab notebooks. The third part, called "Student Handout," includes a reading, a materials list, and data collection procedures.

Table 1.2. Organization of Investigation Lesson Plans

Part #	Section Name	Portions Included
1	Teacher's Lesson Plan Outline	Title, Problem, Prediction Guidelines Notes on Thinking About the Problem Notes on Data Collection and Analysis Expansion and Further Investigation
2	Student Lab Notebook Entries	Title, Problem, Prediction Statements Paraphrased Points on Concepts Data Collection Tables Analysis Questions and Answers Concluding-the-Analysis Statements
3	Student Handout	Title Thinking About the Problem Data Collection Materials List Data Collection Procedures

Anticipatory question. Students begin each lab by being introduced to an anticipatory question. They need to build expectancies for the lab work they will undertake. Students learn better when they are given the opportunity to "wonder" about what they will investigate. For each lesson, the teacher presents the title of the activity and a statement of the problem. The topics and statements chosen reflect the National Science Education Standards and Benchmarks of Science Literacy. This period of initial reflection and class discussion helps students anticipate further information and "whets their appetite" for the investigation that will follow.

Recall of prior knowledge, including misconceptions. Students need to reflect on the topic and make a tentative prediction based on background knowledge they may have, even if the knowledge is very limited. This will help elicit and identify misconceptions. It sets the stage for development of a new equilibrium in their understanding. This process includes the development of skills in anticipation and the formation and refinement of initial hypotheses. The teacher presents a brief on-topic question, about which students write a one-sentence prediction. The finding that their predictions may have been wrong, or in some way lacking, is frequently the best scaffolding and motivation for true concept acquisition.

Defining concepts. Students need accurate input to develop an appreciation for the topic they will investigate. Teachers give students the handout "Thinking About the Problem." This provides generalized content and background information about the investigation that students will be conducting. We suggest that this brief document be read aloud by the teacher with students both listening and following along on their copy. Each student is then required to paraphrase in writing the three most important points of what has been read and heard. Teachers will find this summary of main points from the "Thinking About the Problem" reading to be a valuable scientific-literacy development tool. Throughout the book, this reading includes the etymology of important words. While students should not be expected to know the foreign term, we believe that the inclusion of the root meaning will enhance comprehension and will promote retention of the word itself.

Focusing student lab work. Students need to anticipate the types of data they will observe and measure as a result of the lab work and the general understandings they are trying to obtain. In initial labs, students are allowed to transfer blank data collection tables by drawing them into their notebooks. This helps the students anticipate the type of data they will be asked to provide. In later labs, they will be asked to design their own data collection tables, including their own descriptive titles. In a similar manner, teachers will want to provide a materials list and a set of procedures in the beginning of the school year, and then gradually encourage students to develop their own as the school year progresses. During lab work the role of the teacher is essentially that of a facilitator while students do the hands-on work of collecting data. Rapid progress and enhanced motivation will result when students are given numerous opportunities to collaborate actively with their teacher and one another in a discovery process. Cooperative groups, which involve roles, goals, and specific skills, can be ideal classroom management strategies for these lab groups.

Reporting results and following up. Students need to re-examine the data obtained to analyze and apply what has been learned. They then compose and refine a series of summary statements to accurately report what they have found. The teacher presents the *analysis* questions that are part of the lab, and students answer them in their science lab notebooks. The teacher also uses routine *concluding-the-analysis* statements, with the following sentence starters:

- I learned…

- If I were to re-do this lab, I would change…

- An example of a variable in this lab is…

- An example of a control in this lab is…

Opportunities for differentiation. Students may be required to expand their understanding of the concepts acquired to incorporate new data and/or a larger scope. This further investigation may involve research through internet and library resources. In the "Teacher's Lesson Plan Outline" section of each lab there are expansion questions to facilitate further investigation by students. These expansion questions involve differentiation through not only the higher levels of Bloom's Taxonomy (beyond knowledge and comprehension toward application, analysis, and synthesis) but also Howard Gardner's Theory of Multiple Intelligences (logical/mathematical, verbal/linguistic, visual/spatial, bodily/kinesthetic, naturalistic, interpersonal, musical/rhythmic). The instructional methods are varied, as this enables the students to use their intellectual strengths to better understand topics.

Because rate of learning and ability level normally vary within a given classroom, there are modifications that can be made to the processes of investigation in this book that will be of benefit to special-needs students and others who need extra time or help to effectively comprehend the material and complete the assignment. These include being required to complete a simpler version of each lab report write-up. This write-up would involve reduced amounts of writing, requiring these students only to make a prediction, record the data (in the already prepared data table), and answer analysis questions. Other modifications (such as adjustments to vocabulary load, sentence length, or amount of information to recall) can easily be arranged by the teacher or case manager as the individual classroom situation demands.

Opportunities for applications of various technologies. With each of the labs in this book being divided into three parts, there are corresponding applications of technology possible. In Part 1, the "Teacher's Lesson Plan Outline," extensions could include, but are not limited to, the creation of online learning communities for students. One example is "Moodle," which is a course management system. It is a free, open source software package designed to help educators create effective online learning communities. It can be downloaded and used on any computer. Another example is "Wiki," which is a collection of web pages designed to enable anyone who accesses it to contribute or modify content. Wikis are often used to create collaborative websites and to power community websites. The collaborative encyclopedia called Wikipedia is one of the best-known wikis.

Part 2 of each investigation details the portions of the lab report that will be recorded by students in their lab notebooks. In most classrooms in the 19th and 20th centuries, chalkboards were used; they were eventually joined with the widespread use of overhead projectors. Teachers now have the option of using a much wider variety of technological approaches to project the necessary information. Among the many options are

- SMART Board, an interactive whiteboard that connects to a computer and a digital projector to show the required lab report portions as a computer image. Computer applications can be controlled directly from the display.

- Promethean Activboard, another interactive whiteboard system designed for the classroom.

- Mimio projectors, which can be attached to whiteboards and allow information to be saved to a computer when students report their findings. One can save whiteboard notes in a format that's easy to print, share, or export to the internet.

Part 3 of each investigation is the student handout, which includes the materials list and procedures. A classroom set of laptops can be used with wireless transfers of required information. More advanced methods of data collection can be included in the materials lists, if available. For example, a Vernier LabPro probe is a data collection device that can be used with a computer, a Texas Instruments graphing calculator, Palm handhelds, or on its own as a remote data collector.

Evaluation[1]. As part of the process of investigation featured in this book, each student completes and hands in a lab report (housed within their lab notebooks). These average one per week during the quarter and constitute the major factor in assigning a grade for the course (e.g., based on 30 points per lab). In addition, each student is required to maintain, update, and complete a lab notebook. This is collected and a global grade (e.g., based on 8 points) is assigned once per quarter. Tests, quizzes, class participation, projects, etc., should also be considered when grades are determined, but we suggest that they carry less total weight than the progress shown by students in their lab investigations.

Individual lab reports. Lab reports can be graded according to a 30-point scale when following the "Lab Report Guidelines" (Appendix C, p. 312). All lab reports follow the same framework. Lab reports are made up of the following main headings: anticipation section title, problem, prediction, thinking about the problem, data collection table(s), analysis, and concluding-the-analysis statements (see Table 1.2). Students are also provided with a copy of the "Self-Evaluation Tool" (Appendix C, p. 314). This offers 10 questions for students to ask themselves before submitting any lab report for grading. Students glue this question sheet into their lab notebooks as a reference. Parents have been appreciative when they see this evaluation tool, as it helps them identify questions to ask their children, enabling better accountability.

Feedback. Quick feedback is important for learning. In order to give quick feedback to students, we recommend using class time to grade and return the lab reports. Using the following approach, all of the lab reports for a large class can be graded during one period, while students continue to learn. Students are first told to put a bookmark in their notebooks to identify the beginning of the lab report that is due. All notebooks are then passed forward. While the teacher goes through each book, grading and recording scores, students work on supplementary scientific readings and concept maps; they may also answer analysis section questions for lab reports that later get glued into their notebooks, take quizzes, watch videos that cover the topics of study, and/or read science-related magazines. As with any effective teaching strategy, variety is best.

---

[1]*Note:* The detailed descriptions of the *Evaluation* are meant only as suggestions. The needs and objectives of the individual teacher and of each group of learners will determine what is emphasized and how it is evaluated.

Lab notebook. Composition-style notebooks work best, because they are durable and compact, and students don't tear out any pages. These are inexpensive and widely available at many discount department stores. All pages should be used, both front and back, unless special-needs students have an alternate modification. The first four pages (to be labeled A, G, M, and O to correspond with the major units of study) are for the *Table of Contents.* This helps students monitor, sequence, and organizes their lab reports. The headings in Table 1.3 should be used on each of the A, G, M, and O pages.

Table 1.3. Lab Notebook Table of Contents Framework

Date	Description	Page #

The front cover of the lab notebook should provide a place for students with multiple intelligence strengths in spatial or artistic areas to sketch science-related drawings. A handout is provided to students, to be glued onto their cover, which defines concepts that are studied during the year, along with space for any student artwork (Appendix C, p. 311).

Page one of the lab notebook should be for the students' Taxonomy of Science Words (Table 1.4). Research shows that students perform better on standardized tests when they are familiar with the terms (e.g., *compare and contrast*) used in a broad variety of test questions. Students gradually fill in their taxonomies. Only a few words are added to the grid during the first lab. More terms are added as the year progresses. This will result in the building of a personalized glossary.

Table 1.4. Sample Taxonomy of Science Words

Taxonomy of Science Words	
A: anomaly, astronomy	N:
B: buoyancy	O: observation, oceanography
C: compare, contrast	P: prediction
D:	Q: quantitative, qualitative
E: experiment	R:
F:	S: solid
G: gas, geology	T: taxonomy, temperature
H: hypothesis	U:
I: inference	V:
J:	W:
K:	X:
L: lab, liquid	Y:
M: measure, meteorology	Z:

Page two of the notebook should be the "Lab Notebook Grade Record Sheet" (Table 1.5). This allows students to practice their computation skills, while keeping track of their progress in science.

Table 1.5. Lab Notebook Grade Record Sheet

Assignment Description	Points Earned	Points Possible	Total Points Earned	Total Points Possible	Overall Grade Percentage

Page three of the notebook should be the first page of the individual lab report, including anticipation section title; problem; prediction; etc. (see, above, *individual lab reports*, and, on p. 23, *Lab S-1 Becoming a Scientist*). This page marks the beginning of the students' daily work in science. All *Earth Science Success* lab reports follow a similar framework and progression of learning.

Lab notebooks have proven very effective in helping students stay organized. Large plastic bins can be provided in the classroom, one for each hour, for students to store their notebooks. Students are allowed to bring the notebooks home whenever they choose, but they often prefer to keep them in the science classroom. If students forget their notebooks, they could be required to write any data on a separate blank page, which they later glue into their notebook. Likewise, all graphing is done on separate graph paper and later glued into the notebook. As an added bonus with the notebooks, "no name" papers (when students forget to sign their work) are a thing of the past!

At the end of each quarter, students are given a "Lab Notebook Grading Rubric" (Appendix C, p. 313) to use as a cumulative evaluation tool. The teacher then verifies the student evaluation by checking the notebooks. An extra-credit point can be earned by students who show the notebook and the evaluation tool to a parent or guardian.

The First Ten Days

Note to the Earth Science Teacher: The lesson plans shown below are only suggestions. The needs and objectives of the individual teacher and of each group of learners will determine the pace. Although we have chosen to begin Earth science with astronomy, we believe that teachers can choose to begin with any of the four major topics. It is, however, recommended that the initial investigation be Lab S-1 *Becoming a Scientist.*

Day One

I. Start of the school year

    A. Introductions—Assigning seats on the first day helps the teacher learn student names, place students who need "teacher proximity," and lessen the disappointment inherent in not having a seat near a favorite companion.

    B. Index Card Information—Once data on parent contacts, e-mail addresses, and outside-of-school activities (used to enable motivational conversations during the year) are recorded, index cards can be sorted according to birth dates (utilized to celebrate students' birthdays at the beginning of corresponding class periods). Many software programs, such as Power School, are available to replace index cards for this task, if the teacher prefers.

II. Suggested "break the ice" activities

    A. Earth Science Bingo (Appendix B, p. 268). Students travel around the classroom, in search of someone who has "visited a rock formation while on vacation," "witnessed the launch of a space shuttle," etc., duly noting his/her first name. Students who complete a Bingo get a small prize. All students "win" by learning the names of others.

    B. Lucky Bucket Creation and Drawing—A one-gallon-size bucket is labeled for use in each class period. Students put their first and last names on a small ticket and place it in the "Lucky Bucket." At the beginning of each subsequent class period, one student's name is drawn and she or he is introduced to the class, while receiving a warm round of applause and a small prize (e.g., eraser, sticker). The following day, that student makes a prediction about whose name might be drawn from the bucket ("The new lucky student will have [brown hair, braces, a blue shirt, etc.]"). When the ticket is drawn from the bucket, the new lucky student is now introduced to the class, while receiving a warm round of applause and a small prize. The pattern repeats itself each day, until all names are drawn and new tickets need to be made for the lucky bucket to begin once again.

III. "Predicting the Future" (Appendix B, p. 264). These predictions will be collected and stored in a "time capsule" (file folder) until the end of the school year.

Day Two

I. "Pretest for Earth Science Success" (Appendix B, p. 265)—This pretest covers 33 statements of general knowledge and concepts related to Earth Science. It should not be used to test out-of-core parts of the curriculum. Instead it serves as an advance organizer, helping students anticipate what they will be studying, and allows the teacher to see where the largest gaps are in student understanding.

II. Distribute and discuss "Science Safety Rules" (Appendix C, p. 310). The curriculum and lesson plans in this book are designed to give students hands-on experiences in the sciences in a safe environment. There is no guarantee of safety, however. All science teachers should take steps to provide safe laboratory and field experiences for their students.

III. Develop classroom expectations using "My Job/Your Job" (see p. 11). This management strategy allows for student "buy-in," while expectations, well-known by middle school students, are reinforced by their teacher. Students begin by defining "My Job" as any task the students feel must be performed by the teacher, so that the classroom will have a good learning environment during the school year. In a similar manner, students define "Your Job" as those tasks that they themselves must perform for the learning environment to be successful. Each class is encouraged to brainstorm two or three new jobs for the list, so that by the end of the day, the complete list can be posted in the room and shared with all. By including student feedback and the teacher's positive "catch-all" rephrasing—such as, "respect the rights and feelings of others"—students are given ownership of the rules and expectations. Students will be held more accountable for their own behaviors and for the behaviors of their peers. The list is reviewed each quarter (or when situations prove necessary), to make sure that all are reminded of the jobs that were agreed upon. Figure 1.1 shows a sample list, developed by the author's students. It is evident that a few of the rules were borrowed from other students while brainstorming.

Figure 1.1. My Job/Your Job

My Job:

Teach

Work hard

Get graded papers back quickly

Make science fun

Give out prizes (when earned!)

Be fair with due dates

No singing (except for birthdays)

Keep hands, feet, and all objects to myself

Your Job:

Learn

Work hard

Do work on time

Keep hands, feet, and all objects to ourselves

Listen

Act happy (no whining, griping, etc. allowed)

Use courtesy laughter with all of your teacher's attempts at humor

Be respectful of others

IV. Lucky Bucket Drawing (see Day One: II.B, page 9) gets repeated daily.

Day Three

I. Explain and demonstrate the "KWL Flip Book on Astronomy"—KWL stands for "Know, Want to know, and Learn." This flip book is two sheets of copy paper folded over each other (see Illustration 1.1). The outer sheet is folded one-third of the way down the paper. The inner sheet is folded to within one inch of the bottom edge. When the two sheets are fitted together, they form a four-page flip book. On the top page, students write their name and the word *astronomy* in large lettering. On the second page, along the bottom edge, where it can be read when the book is closed, students write, "What do I know?" On the third page, also along the bottom edge, students write, "What do I want to know?" On the final page, students write, "What did I learn?" along the bottom edge. To begin, students fill in at least five facts that they know about astronomy, without hints from the teacher. (Assure them that it is okay if they end up being wrong.) Students also fill in at least two topics that they would like to learn more about. The flip books are then handed in, so the teacher can evaluate background knowledge of students, without attaching a grade. On the last day of the quarter, after having spent time learning astronomy concepts, students fill in 10 things that they learned. It is often interesting (and provides a rich environment for discussion) to see that some "facts" that students thought they knew in the beginning of the quarter actually ended up being incorrect.

Illustration 1.1. Flip Book on Astronomy

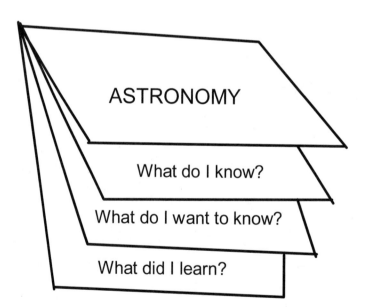

II. Begin the setting up of the Science Lab Notebook (see p. 6, Evaluation)

III. *Anticipation.* Begin Lab S-1 "Becoming a Scientist" (p. 23).

A. "Anticipation Section Title" and "Problem" are provided, by projector, for students to record in their notebooks. This investigation introduces students to the nature of scientific inquiry, which establishes the idea that scientific information is gathered from observations of phenomena. Introducing students to laboratory investigations helps build an atmosphere in which students are members of a research team investigating events in a search for explanations. The *Title* of this lab is "Becoming a Scientist." Students observe a large glass cylinder with pink fluid in it. They see three small tubes, each filled with a different amount of blue fluid. They learn that the three small tubes will soon be dropped into the large cylinder. The problem is, "What is it that scientists look for when they make great discoveries?"

B. Students are invited to speculate on a "Prediction" about what scientists look for during investigations. For Lab S-1, they are told: "Describe, in one sentence, your answer to the problem statement." Students are then expected to write a complete sentence, making an educated guess about the problem. It may be helpful to inform students that there is research that shows that concepts are best learned by first wondering about them. This is why we suggest that students be graded only on effort and completion for this portion of the lab report, not on accuracy.

C. Distribute the Lab S-1 student handout (p. 30), allotting time to carefully read the "Thinking About the Problem" section. It is also important to allow time for students to paraphrase three main points in their notebooks. This section gives background concepts and invites discussion of vocabulary, such as *inference, observation,* and *anomaly.* These words can be entered into the students' "Taxonomy of Science Words" page. It also helps students identify the main ideas when they are encouraged to underline particular words in the "Thinking About the Problem" section that are referred to during the discussion.

D. "Data collection tables" are transferred into student notebooks. Students are allowed to transfer blank data collection tables by drawing them into their notebooks, helping the students to anticipate the type of data they will be asked to provide. Students must analyze what they see in each data collection table. The first data collection table shows the three different tubes, one cylinder on which a prediction is drawn, and one cylinder on which an actual observation will be drawn.

Day Four

I. Data collection.

    A. Encourage students to make verbal observations (both "qualitative" and "quantitative"). Enable them to make these detailed observations by using the example of each student's right hand. Solicit qualitative descriptions of the right hand (shape, texture, color, features, etc.) and quantitative descriptions (e.g., finger length, width, quantity of knuckles, mass of rings). Then, after students have drawn the first data collection table, they are shown the actual materials. Students are now able to make detailed visual observations and written predictions about (the cylinder of fluids) and the blue tubes, using Data Collection Table #1 to draw and label their prediction (p. 28).

    It does not take long for students to see (the line between the two pink fluids in the cylinder.) They are not told the fact that the fluids are lamp oil and slightly salty water. If, after their observations, students can make inferences as to what the fluids are, this should not be discouraged, but verification for accuracy should wait until students have completed the lab work.

    B. After predictions are recorded in lab notebooks, a demonstration is done by the teacher to show the actual results. One blue tube after another is dropped into the cylinder. After dropping each tube into the cylinder, students draw and label the actual results. This invariably causes a puzzling situation, when students are confronted with anomalies regarding what they expected (e.g., tube 2 sinks to the bottom of the cylinder, while tube 1 floats at the barrier between the two fluids in the cylinder). At this stage, students have a natural, and relatively urgent, desire to want to work with the equipment and find answers to their questions. Teachers can encourage this by showing students the smaller cylinders of pink fluids and the smaller blue tubes that they will be using. At each station in the lab, the students are supplied with empty tubes and with access to the three different fluids, named simply 1, 2, and 3. Anomalies are wonderful for engaging students' curiosity and motivating inquiry. Enthusiasm builds in the room, as students are shown the key to getting to work with the equipment…that being the completion of Data Collection Table #2 (p. 28).

II. Begin Lab S-1 "Becoming a Scientist" data collection

    A. Working in small groups, students must come to agreement on a hypothesis (an explanation that can be tested) about what happened and record this in their individual lab notebooks. Teachers should avoid telling students what the fluids are, because the lack of information ends up inspiring further investigations. The fluids in the tubes all have the same blue food coloring in them, but they are all different fluids (water, saturated Epsom salt solution, and isopropyl alcohol). Due to their differences in density, a smaller amount of blue fluid can actually float above a larger quantity of blue fluid, when housed in a small tube.

Students put on aprons, goggles, and work in small groups to develop a hypothesis about why any particular anomaly is occurring. The goal is to encourage students to see themselves as members of a scientific team, investigating physical phenomena in search of explanations of unexplained situations. In this approach, their teacher is a "research supervisor," promoting safety and providing equipment for their ideas, rather than someone who dictates what students must discover. However, it is vital to check and approve all student-designed experiments for safety before they are performed.

B. Each student then sketches and labels the group's idea for an experiment that will test their hypothesis into Data Collection Table #2 in their lab notebook. Once they have agreed, as a team, to the first explanation they will test (hypothesis), they must obtain the required materials from their teacher and begin to collect data.

C. Students record any hypotheses, experiments, and results on Data Collection Table #2. Class ends with each student submitting an "exit card" (Figure 1.2) to the assignment collection basket. On this index card, he or she records brief answers to three questions. Students are given the three questions and the index card midway through their lab work in class. This card is returned, with a grade on it, the following day. This process of reflection and writing will help sharpen critical thinking skills. If available, the use of Clicker Technology, also known as Student Response Systems, can enable the recording of feedback and rapid projection of responses as a replacement for exit cards. As a caution, however, multiple-choice questions will need to be written to replace open-ended questions to implement the use of this technology.

Figure 1.2. Sample Exit Card

Exit Card

Name _____

One new thing I learned today is…

One idea that I really understand is…

One question I still have is…

Day Five

I. "Becoming a Scientist" data collection continues.

    D. Students conduct more experiments to test different hypotheses by following procedures #3–5 on their handout (p. 31). This will require at least one full class period, possibly two at the teacher's discretion, devoted to running experiments and recording results, in order to satisfy students' curiosity about this particular investigation.

    E. Students present their best results to the class, sharing hypotheses, strategies attempted, and findings. Sketches of their investigation materials, plus brief descriptions of what their "best" discovery means, are shared by the team with the whole class.

Day Six

I. Distribute and discuss the "Lab Report Guidelines" (Appendix C, p. 312). Students learn about the requirements for the "Concluding-The-Analysis" section on the lab report. We believe that these conclusion statements are vital for students to learn basic laboratory procedures as well as more complex thinking skills in science.

II. Set the "Becoming a Scientist" lab report due date for Day Nine. We suggest that teachers reserve a small, yet permanent, section of the chalkboard for "planner notes" (masking tape makes nice lines on a chalkboard that are not erased on a daily basis). In this planner space are written due dates for upcoming science assignments. A labeled space for English, math, social studies, etc. assignments is provided, as well. Students fill in the information from other team classes as the day progresses.

III. "Analysis." Students transfer the Lab S-1 "Analysis" questions into their notebooks, and work on completing their responses with detail and accuracy (p. 29). The "Analysis" questions guide the students' summary and interpretation of results from the investigation. The questions are based on data analysis and generalizations derived from the experiment.

There are basically four steps to the framework presented in this laboratory investigation. The first is the identification of the anomaly. Students try to decide exactly what was going on when they witnessed the unexpected event. The second is hypothesis formation and testing. In this step students decide what might be a good explanation for a portion of the events. The third step is analysis and labeling of concepts, during which students decide which explanation their small group agrees on and what they should call that agreed-upon explanation. The final step involves generalized testing and application, where students might extend their investigation into what would happen in other cases. If one group does not get as far as the next, they can see the potential for further investigation when they hear the other groups' summary presentations. Finally, students check their lab reports against the assessment rubric and the "Self-Evaluation Tool" handouts (Appendix C, p. 314). Students review their individual lab report from Lab S-1 to see if they can answer "yes" to each of the ten questions.

IV. Preview any outside reading assignment for this quarter (e.g., from handouts and/or supplementary textbooks). Outside reading assignments can take many forms, from textbook chapters to current events articles related to the topics of study. In the case of a textbook, if there are enough copies for individual students to each take one, we recommend that it be used for outside-of-class homework. Chapters can be assigned one per month, which tie into the lessons covered during the school day. A quiz can be given to assess the students' knowledge of the concepts covered in the particular chapter. If, however, only one classroom set of textbooks is available, they can be used as handy reference materials to enrich any lesson with their diagrams, glossaries, and extensive background information. In the absence of textbooks, newspapers, news magazines, and internet sites with coverage of current events can serve as a wealth of information on Earth science–related topics.

Day Seven

I. Anticipation. Begin Lab A-1 "Sizing Up the Planets" (Chapter 2, p. 37). Now that students are more familiar with the thinking patterns and the nature of scientific investigations, we begin our first astronomy lab.

    A. "Anticipation Section Title" and "Problem" are provided for students to record in their notebooks. The title for this first astronomy lab is "Sizing Up the Planets." There are two ways to think about scale sizes in the solar system (the solar system is defined as consisting of the Sun and all of the objects that revolve around it). One is the size of the individual planets, and the other is how far apart the planets are from one another. Both of these concepts involve many misconceptions by students (and teachers!), so both should be dealt with, back-to-back, in the lesson planning sequence. Both also deal with current events in the news—for example, the fact that it has been determined that Pluto is no longer among those considered "classical planets." Therefore, the statement of the problem for this lab is "How big are the planets?" Once this is written in the students' lab notebooks, the teacher provides a labeled list (see Figure 1.3), which students are required to transfer into their notebooks.

    As with all of science, concepts presented as "facts" are subject to change as new information becomes better understood by scientists. Figure 1.3 may also be subject to change. Discussion on this topic can provide both a learning opportunity for students and a research challenge for the newest definitions of *classical, dwarf,* and *plutoid* planets.

    B. Labeled sketch of some objects in our solar system

Figure 1.3. Some Objects in Our Solar System

- Sun
- Mercury – Classical Planet
- Venus – Classical Planet
- Earth – Classical Planet
- Mars – Classical Planet
- Ceres – Dwarf Planet (formerly an asteroid)
- Jupiter – Classical Planet
- Saturn – Classical Planet
- Uranus – Classical Planet

- Neptune – Classical Planet

- Pluto – Plutoid (formerly considered a planet, then a dwarf planet)

- Charon – Dwarf Planet (formerly a moon of Pluto)

- Eris – Plutoid Planet (a trans-Neptunian object in the Kuiper Belt, whose discovery caused the redefinition of planets)

C. Students are invited to speculate on a "Prediction" about how the Earth compares with the Sun in terms of size. On the projector is written, "Describe how you think the Earth compares with the Sun in terms of size." After students are finished writing their predictions, we suggest that you remind them of the hanging mobiles that were once popular. Many misconceptions about the solar system arise from classroom decorations by teachers and bedroom decorations in the students' homes. Show students a large yellow beach ball, telling them that this will be the model Sun for the lab. Ask students to show how big the Earth would be in comparison. Ask them to remember what they originally thought, because it will play an important role in how much they learn during this investigation.

II. Do the "Petals Around Roses" activity. In this activity, five dice are used to show students a critical-thinking puzzle to solve. In advance, take digital pictures of the rolls of five dice for use with your projector, or roll five dice onto a photocopier and make a transparency of each result. (It is helpful to have at least five different dice-roll images.) Show students the first image and ask them, "How many petals around the roses are there?" The typical response is "huh?" followed quickly by a guess from a student. They often start by thinking that the total number shown on all of the dice should determine the answer. The game was developed by Bill Gates and the actual answer involves knowing what a "rose" is and what a "petal" is. In this game, a *rose* is defined as a roll of 1, 3, or 5 because each of those rolls has a center dot, around which "petals" can be shown (see Illustration 1.2). Two "petals" are shown on this example, because a roll of three has a center dot, making it a "rose." After most students begin catching on, explain the answer to the rest, and then move on with Lab A-1.

Illustration 1.2. Petals Around Roses

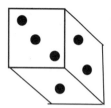

A. Distribute the Lab A-1 handout (Chapter 2, pp. 41–42), allotting time to carefully read the "Thinking About the Problem" section. Allow time also for students to paraphrase the three main points in their notebooks. The reading can be used with literacy teaching strategies to encourage the finding and paraphrasing of main ideas.

B. The "Data Collection Tables" are transferred into student notebooks. Having students draw the data collection tables encourages them to anticipate data that may be important during the investigation.

Day Eight

I. Data collection. Begin and complete Lab A-1 "Sizing Up the Planets" laboratory investigation work (Chapter 2, page 38).

A. The "Data Collection Materials" and "Procedures" are shown on the student handout. An explanation of the materials and procedures that are used is given to students. Their first task is to brainstorm, in small groups, about how to find the diameter of the model Sun (a large yellow beach ball), recording it in their notebooks. Many try to measure the circumference, but forget the equation that relates it to diameter. Many more try quick, inaccurate measurement techniques. If students do not come within 0.5 cm of the actual measurement, I tell them to go "back to the drawing board." Soon, they realize that the height of the ball above ground (equivalent to its diameter) can be quite accurately measured with a meter stick, provided a lab partner can hold a steady ruler across the top of the beach ball.

B. Students next use the model Sun's diameter to calculate the Comparison Constant (CC.) The CC is a ratio that is equal to the model Sun diameter divided by 109 (due to the fact that 109 Earths can fit across the midline of the Sun). This equation, Model Sun Diameter ÷ 109 = CC, is used to figure out the Comparison Diameters for each planet. The data collection table is used to calculate each of the Planet Model Diameters. Students multiply (without a calculator, for best practice in interdisciplinary math computation) the Comparison Diameter (given in Data Collection Table #1) by the CC to get the Planet Model Diameter.

C. Students draw and label each planet from their data tables, in their lab notebooks, to show Planet Model sizes. Some reteaching may be necessary about how to use a ruler to measure small diameters (e.g., 0.35 centimeters). It is very useful to have a transparent plastic ruler and to use it on an overhead projector to demonstrate some of these measurement techniques.

D. As a group, students find, modify, or make an object (wadded up newspapers and masking tape) with the required diameter in centimeters for each planet. Students bring their collections of planets near the model Sun. They should soon learn that, compared with the model Sun, Earth is barely visible. They also begin to notice the many inaccuracies in the solar system mobiles that hang in classrooms. Many of those mobiles show the Earth as being fairly close in size to the Sun, when in fact it is not close at all.

Day Nine

I. Correction of Lab S-1 "Becoming a Scientist." Lab notebooks are collected for correction and grading. At the beginning of class, ask students to use a piece of scrap paper to bookmark the front page of their Lab S-1 report. They then hand the notebooks forward for collection. This prevents some students from gaining unfair additional work time on their lab reports due to positioning in the classroom. All reports are submitted for grading in random order. There is ample opportunity to have students witness the grading, as individuals, in a semiprivate conference with their teacher, if they choose. When a lab notebook has been graded and recorded, it should be returned to the storage bin where students can retrieve it. The authors have found that, due to this method, students eagerly view their assessment feedback.

II. Analysis. During the correction time, students work on the "Analysis" questions and "Concluding-The-Analysis" statements from *Lab A-1* "Sizing Up the Planets" (Chapter 2, p. 40) on a separate sheet of paper. Once answered, the questions can be glued into lab notebooks on the appropriate page. Students also read "Scale Model Wonderings" (Figure 1.4). This is a series of five questions designed to help students build an understanding of extremely large numbers. The questions are phrased to show students comparisons with objects they can relate to, dimension-wise. Students can be asked to develop their own scale model comparisons, using a favorite object, as well.

Figure 1.4. Scale Model Wonderings

1. Have you been alive for 1,000,000 minutes?

>Yes. 1,000,000 minutes = 1.9 years.

2. If you wanted to travel 1,000,000 centimeters, should you walk, drive, or go by plane?

>Drive. 1,000,000 cm = 10 km. That's a possible distance to walk, but most students would opt to drive. Flying is a possibility, but it is not a reasonable choice.

3. If you won $1,000,000 in a lottery, and you got paid in $1 bills, could you lift and carry your winnings to the bank?

>No. A single dollar bill weighs about one gram. But 1,000,000 dollar bills would weigh over one metric ton, which would be much too heavy for one person to carry.

4. Would 1,000,000 grains of rice fit into a two-liter bottle?

>No. About 20,000 grains of rice fit into a two-liter bottle.

5. Would 1,000,000 mL of water be enough to fill a backyard swimming pool?

>Yes. 1,000,000 mL of water would be approximately what is needed to fill the pool.

Day Ten

I. Review the procedures with students for the "Panel of Five" game (Appendix B, p. 269). There are several ways in which a teacher can use an article from a publication to enhance classroom instruction. One of those ways is a game called Panel of Five, which has proven to be very popular, and successful as an instructional tool, with early adolescents. Use "The Legend of Orion the Hunter" (Appendix B) for this first game so that students can develop good game skills while learning about an astronomy-related legend. As with all instructional strategies, variety is the best policy.

Lab Science 1: (S-1) Becoming a Scientist

Part 1: (Teacher's Lesson Plan Outline)

Note: See the applicable cross-references for the National Science Standards and Benchmarks for Science Literacy for this lab in the introduction, (pp. xiii-xvi).

Anticipation Section Title: (S-1) Becoming a Scientist

Problem: What is it that scientists look for when they make great discoveries?

Prediction: Describe, in one sentence, your answer to the problem statement. *Note:* Have students write their prediction prior to giving them the handout.

Thinking About the Problem: (Read aloud by teacher from the student handout and then paraphrased by students in lab notebooks.)

Note: Students prepare for data collection by drawing, or attaching, *data tables* and writing *analysis* section questions (see *Part 2*).

Data Collection Materials and Procedures: (Review using the student handout prior to beginning data collection.)

Note: Appendix A has a complete list of materials.
Note: Lists of all the necessary materials for the demonstration by the teacher are on page 24.

The student set (designed for groups of three to four) is a smaller version of the teacher demonstration and consists of a 100 mL graduated cylinder; three glass test tubes (0.5 dram); and the fluids (see Table 1.6, p. 28).

- 250 mL glass cylinder

- 150 mL partially saturated saltwater

- 100 mL lamp oil

- 3 test tubes, 75 mm x 10 mm

- 3 corks, #1

- 50 mL water

- 50 mL saturated Epsom salt solution (700 g of Epsom salt in 1000 mL of water)

- 50 mL isopropyl alcohol

- Eye droppers

- Coat hanger wire (for bending into tube-retrieval hooks)

- 250 mL beakers

Safety Requirements: goggles, aprons

Available Resources for Experiments:

- Beakers

- Fluids from tubes 1, 2, and 3

- Water from sink

Lab Rules and Requirements (to post and explain):

- Do not alter or change the tubes or corks systems.

- For any other equipment in room, ask first.

- Do not taste or directly smell anything.

- Goggles and aprons are to be worn at all times.

- After lab, wash hands, equipment, and lab counter. Return equipment neatly and carefully.

Expansion and Further Investigation:

(1) Answer the following questions in complete sentences: What do you think is the best hypothesis (explanation) about why tube 2 sinks to the bottom of the cylinder? What evidence do you have to support this hypothesis (explanation)? Is it possible that your best hypothesis is incorrect? Explain.

(2) How could you sink a small jar in a bucket of water so that only half of it is submerged? Test and explain what you did and how you did it.

Note: (Extra for Lab S-1) In this first lab of the school year, it is possible that groups may need a few suggestions when they try to generate hypotheses in step 3 of the Data Collection Procedures. The following samples are provided in case teachers need to give "helpful hints."

Sample Hypothesis #1: The tubes are different.

Sample Experiment Design #1:

(1) Take three empty tubes from the cart.

(2) Clean and dry the tubes.

(3) Place each tube on a triple beam balance and measure the mass.

(4) Use a ruler to measure the dimensions of each tube.

(5) Record your results.

Sample Hypothesis #2: Tube 2 and tube 3 are the same liquid.

Sample Experiment Design #2:

(1) Weigh a graduated cylinder.

(2) Pour exactly 30 mL of fluid #2 into the graduated cylinder.

(3) Weigh the graduated cylinder again, determining the exact weight of the fluid.

(4) Repeat this sequence for fluid #3.

(5) Record your results.

Part 2: (Student Lab Notebook Entries)

Note: In this first lab, typical responses have been added to show examples of student lab notebook entries.

Anticipation Section Title: (S-1) Becoming a Scientist

Problem: What is it that scientists look for when they make great discoveries?

Prediction: Answer the problem statement

(Example): *I think they look for…*

Note: Distribute the student handout (see *Part 3*) after students have completed their prediction.

Thinking About the Problem: Paraphrase the three main points of the reading in your own words.

(1) (Example): *Scientists have made many great discoveries just by being curious enough to investigate things they observe.*

(2) (Example): *An inference is our explanation for what we are observing.*

(3) (Example): *An anomaly is an unexpected event that can teach us a lot if we investigate it.*

Table 1.6. Data Collection Table #1: Anticipation Demo

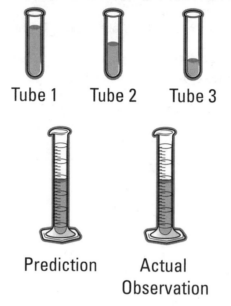

Tube 1   Tube 2   Tube 3

Prediction   Actual
Observation

Note: In initial labs, students are allowed to transfer blank data collection tables by drawing them into their notebooks. This helps the students anticipate the type of data they will be asked to provide. In later labs, they can be asked to design their own data collection tables, such as Table 1.7 below.

Table 1.7. Data Collection Table #2: Small Group Experiments for Lab S-1

HYPOTHESIS (EXPLANATION THAT CAN BE TESTED)	EXPERIMENT (LABELED SKETCH OF OBSERVATION)	EXPLANATION (WHAT YOUR RESULTS MEAN, IN WORDS)

Analysis:

(1) What is causing the tubes to end up where they do?

(Example): *I think the weight of the fluid in each tube is causing it to end up floating in a particular spot inside the cylinder.*

(2) Which observations were easiest to explain?

(Example): *The easiest observation to explain was the line I saw in the middle of the pink cylinder. It is there because there are two different fluids in it, floating on each other.*

(3) Describe the new information you learned from each experiment.

(Example): *In the first, I learned that the three blue fluids are not all the same. In the second, I learned that tube 3 does not smell like mouthwash. In the third, I learned that tube 1 is not fingernail polish remover.*

(4) When a scientist sees an anomaly, what is the best way to go about understanding or explaining it?

(Example): *The scientist should come up with a hypothesis that explains something about it and then do an experiment to test the hypothesis.*

Concluding-the-Analysis Statements:

(1) I learned…

(Example): *I learned that some fluids can float on other fluids.*

(2) If I were to re-do this lab, I would change…

(Example): *If I were to redo this lab, I would add baby oil to the big cylinder to see where the tubes floated in that fluid.*

(3) An example of a variable in this lab is…

(Example): *A variable in this experiment is the type of blue fluid in each tube.*

(4) An example of a control in this lab is…

(Example): *A control in this experiment is the size of each tube.*

Part 3: (Student Handout)

Note: Distribute to students after they complete the *Prediction* in *Part 2*. See also the NSTA website, where there is a link to *Earth Science Success* resources.

Anticipation Section Title: (S-1) Becoming a Scientist

Thinking About the Problem

What do scientists do? Scientists are a bit like detectives. Scientists and detectives try to find out why events happen and they both start with an investigation. This process involves close observation of the facts, making inferences about what was observed, developing an explanation that can be tested, and conducting experiments to see if the hypothesis (*hupotithenai*, "to guess" in Greek) turns out to be true. This method has often led detectives to solve crimes; it has also led scientists to exciting and valuable discoveries.

Scientific investigation for you, in this course, will involve observation, inference, and experimentation to see if your hypotheses are correct. This process can be repeated in case additional experimentation is needed if your hypotheses are found not to be correct.

Your first step in each scientific investigation will always be close and careful observation. Observations are simply information taken in through our five senses. Occasionally this leads to an anomaly. An anomaly (*a + homos*, "not the same" in Greek) means that something unexpected has happened. Scientists often learn much from anomalies.

Based on your observations, you will then make inferences. These involve using your observations to try to come up with an explanation, an educated guess. An inference is therefore your interpretation or explanation of what you observed. This leads you toward formulating a hypothesis, which is an explanation that can be tested in an experiment.

In this first lab, you will experiment with different containers and fluids. Observe carefully what happens. You are encouraged to make educated guesses about your observations, trying to determine which can easily be explained and which cannot. Be especially alert for anomalies that you observe.

Data Collection Materials:

- Empty tubes with corks
- Set of fluids and tubes

Data Collection Procedures: (Step-by-step instructions for student lab work)

(1) Make verbal observations and predictions about the cylinder of fluids and the tubes. Using Data Collection Table #1, draw and label your prediction.

(2) After your teacher does the demonstration, draw and label the actual results.

(3) As a small lab group, come to agreement on a hypothesis (an easily testable explanation for one of the observations you made) about what happened.

(4) Sketch and label an experiment to test your hypothesis.

(5) Record all hypotheses, experiments, and results on Data Collection Table #2.

(6) Conduct more experiments to test different hypotheses by following procedures 3–5.

(7) Present your best results to the class.

LESSON PLANNING

Initial classroom procedures recommended in this book are common to all the investigations (labs). They are therefore listed below to provide a useful reference point when teachers are planning their classes. Words in bold are the headings found in each of the labs in the four chapters that follow.

Part 1: Teacher's Lesson Plan Outline

(1) Review applicable cross-references for the National Science Education Standards and Benchmarks for Science Literacy for this lab in the Introduction (pp. xiii–xvi).

(2) Begin by telling students the **Title** and **Problem** for the lab.

(3) Encourage students to reflect on these and to share what they may already know or believe about the topic. Discuss misconceptions and review relevancy of the topic to what they have seen and heard.

(4) Show students the **Prediction**, and have them write a one-sentence response to complete the **Prediction** in their notebooks, before they receive any handouts.

(5) After students complete the **Prediction** provide them with a copy of the handout **Thinking About the Problem.** We suggest that teachers read this aloud while students follow on their copies.

(6) Require students to write three sentences to paraphrase what they believe to be three main concepts in **Thinking About the Problem.** They write these main points in their notebooks, using their own words.

(7) Review the **Data Collection Materials** and **Procedures**, found on the student handouts, prior to beginning data collection. Students prepare for data collection by drawing, or attaching, data tables and writing analysis section questions (see *Part 2* of each lab).

Part 2: Student Lab Notebook Entries

We recommend the use of a projector for data tables and analysis questions.

Note: Appendix A contains a complete list of materials.

Part 3: Student Handouts

The NSTA website has a link to *Earth Science Success* resources. There you will find an electronic version of the student handouts that facilitates personalization and reproduction.

Chapter 2

Astronomy

*N*ote to the teacher: Our teaching suggestions, found in "The First Ten Days" (chapter 1), include the first of the astronomy labs. In the astronomy unit, students investigate techniques that are used to measure distances, as well as the large-magnitude sizes of objects found in the solar system. Students begin to understand many features of our planet that make it unique and habitable. Students use this information to place the Earth in relation to the Sun and other planets. Students perform activities that focus on comparisons between Earth and other planets, showing why Earth maybe the only planet that currently sustains life. Through labs, as well as enrichment opportunities in each, students are confronted with several areas of planetary astronomy about which people have misconceptions.

Table 2.1. Possible Syllabus for the First Ten Days of Astronomy

Week 1	Day 1	Day 2	Day 3	Day 4	Day 5
	Initial activities, "Predicting the Future" activity	Earth Science pretest, "Science Safety Rules"	KWL flip book, begin Lab S-1 (anticipation)	Lab S-1 (begin data collection)	Lab S-1 (finish data collection, share findings)
Week 2	**Day 1**	**Day 2**	**Day 3**	**Day 4**	**Day 5**
	Lab S-1 (analysis)	Lab A-1 (anticipation), "Petals Around Roses" (p. 19)	Lab A-1 (data collection)	Lab S-1 (report due), Lab A-1 (analysis)	"Panel of Five" ("The Legend of Orion the Hunter")

Lab Astronomy 1: (A-1) Sizing Up the Planets

Part 1: (Teacher's Lesson Plan Outline)

Note: See Lesson Planning on page 32.

Anticipation Section Title: (A-1) Sizing Up the Planets

Problem: How big are the planets?

Prediction: Describe how you think the Earth compares to the Sun in terms of size.

Thinking About the Problem: (See p. 41.)

Data Collection Materials and Procedures: (See p. 42.)

Expansion and Further Investigation:

(1) Measure the circumference of our model Sun. Use the formula, $D = C \div \pi$, to calculate its diameter, where "D" is the diameter, "C" is the circumference, and "π" is the constant 3.14. Is the value for the Sun's diameter, which you calculated here, the same value as that obtained in procedure #1 (p. 42)? Explain any differences.

(2) Calculate the relative volumes of all of the planets and the Sun, compared with the volume of Earth. Use the comparison diameters given in Data Collection Table #1 to calculate the volume of each sphere: $\frac{4}{3} \pi r^3$. How do your calculations compare with the statement that the Sun contains more than one million times as much volume as the Earth?

(3) Find out all you can about our newest dwarf and plutoid planets and the Kuiper Belt (where most are located). Share your findings with the class.

SCI LINKS.
THE WORLD'S A CLICK AWAY
Topic: Planets
Go to: *www.scilinks.org*
Code: ESS001

Part 2: (Student Lab Notebook Entries)

Anticipation Section Title: (A-1) Sizing Up the Planets

Problem: How big are the planets?

Prediction:

Note: Distribute the student handout (see *Part 3*) after students have completed their predictions.

Thinking About the Problem: Paraphrase the three main points of the reading in your own words.

(1)

(2)

(3)

Table 2.2. Sketch for Procedure #5

Table 2.3. Data Collection Table #1: Model Comparison Diameters

Planet Type	Comparison Diameter	Comparison Constant	Planet Model Diameter
"Classical Planets" (Large enough to be dominant over smaller bodies in their paths)			
Mercury	0.38		
Venus	0.95		
Earth	1.00		
Mars	0.53		
Jupiter	11.20		
Saturn	9.50		
Uranus	4.00		
Neptune	3.90		
"Dwarf Planets" (Larger diameter objects, not considered classical planets)			
Ceres	0.08		
Charon	0.10		
"Plutoids" (Larger in mass than "dwarf planets")			
Pluto	0.19		
Eris	0.29		

Note: Actual diameters of solar system objects are: Sun 1,392,000 km; Mercury 4,878 km; Venus 12,102 km; Earth 12,756 km; Mars 6,794 km; Jupiter 142,984 km; Saturn 120,536 km; Uranus 51,118 km; Neptune 49,528 km; Ceres 940 km; Charon 1,172 km; Pluto 2,300 km; and Eris 2,400 km.

Analysis:

(1) How many times larger is the diameter of the largest planet than the diameter of the smallest?

(2) Rank the planets (classical, dwarf, and plutoid) from largest to smallest.

(3) Describe in detail how the Earth compares with the Sun, in terms of size.

(4) Describe two of the most important observations you made when you brought your collection of planets near the model Sun.

Concluding-the-Analysis Statements:

(1) I learned…

(2) If I were to re-do this lab, I would change…

(3) An example of a variable in this lab is…

(4) An example of a control in this lab is…

Part 3: (Student Handout)

Note: Distribute to students after they complete the Prediction in *Part 2*.

Anticipation Section Title: (A-1) Sizing Up the Planets

Thinking About the Problem

What do astronomers do? The word *astronomy* (*astron*, "star" in Greek) means literally "the study of stars" and human beings have been gazing in wonder at the sky for a very long time. Careful observations by ancient scientists are what helped reveal "tricks" or "patterns" that explain events in the night sky. These ancient stargazers were from many different cultures, including the Greeks, the Romans, and the Mayans. They developed myths to explain events associated with things they did not understand (movements of the stars and planets, for example). Very careful observers from these cultures were able to explain things mathematically with reliability, predictability, and precision. It helped that there was far less light pollution long ago, which makes the stars harder for us to see today. These observers formulated testable hypotheses and science was born!

One observation that you could make is that Earth seems very large. Yet, Earth is dwarfed by our immense Sun. Earth, with its 12,756-kilometer diameter, is still 109 times smaller than the Sun. Even Jupiter, the largest planet, is only about one-tenth the Sun's diameter. And Pluto, recently defined as a plutoid, is almost 600 times smaller than the Sun.

Processes and conditions that were at work during the formation of the solar system (*sol*, "sun" in Latin) about 5 billion years ago formed the planets into the sizes that we now observe. The four largest planets (Jupiter, Saturn, Uranus, and Neptune) contain enormous amounts of hydrogen and helium. Earth, and the other smaller planets, do not contain nearly as much of these gases. The quantities of these gases affect how large a planet can become. You will investigate this further in Lab A-4.

In this lab, you will develop your own scale model of the planets to learn about their relative sizes, compared with the Sun.

Data Collection Materials:

- Calculator

- Metric ruler

- Model Sun (one for entire class)

- Newspaper

- One meter of masking tape

Data Collection Procedures:

(1) Find the diameter of our model Sun: ___ cm

(2) Use the model Sun's diameter to calculate the Comparison Constant (CC) below. You will use the CC to figure out the diameters for each planet model.

Model Sun Diameter ÷ 109 = CC

___ cm ÷ 109 = ___

(3) Use Data Collection Table #1 to calculate the Planet Model Diameters for each planet. Multiply the Comparison Diameter by the CC to get the diameter for each planet model. Use only two decimal places in your answer.

(4) For each planet, use wadded-up newspaper and tape to make a model with the required diameter.

(5) Bring your collection of planets near the model Sun. Draw and label the planets, showing planet model sizes.

Lab Astronomy 2: (A-2) Estimating With Metrics

Part 1: (Teacher's Lesson Plan Outline)

Note: See Lesson Planning on page 32. We believe that this lab is especially appropriate for the integration of STEM (Science, Technology, Engineering, and Mathematics).

Anticipation Section Title: (A-2) Estimating With Metrics

Problem: Which equipment is best when measuring amounts of liquid? Of solids?

Prediction: Describe, in one sentence, how you would measure a solid differently from a liquid.

Thinking About the Problem: (See p. 48.)

Data Collection Materials and Procedures: (See p. 49.)

Note: The correct answers to analysis question #3 (p. 47): Length of a football field: C. 90 m; Height of a woman: B. 160 cm; Width of a room: C. 8 m; Width of a desk: B. 75 cm; Mass of a dog: C. 8 kg; Mass of a pencil: B. 5 g; Mass of a raisin: B. 1 g; Mass of an adult: C. 60 kg; Volume of a car gas tank: B. 8 L; Volume of a coffee cup: A. 250 mL; Volume of bathtub: D. 40 L; Volume of a pop can: A. 500 mL; Temperature of boiling water: A. 100°C; Temperature of ice: A. 0°C; Room temperature: A. 22°C; and Body temperature: B. 37°C.

Safety Requirements: goggles, aprons

Expansion and Further Investigation:

(1) Find the equivalents for the following metric units for mass.

1 kg = ___ g = ___ mg

.001 kg = ___ g = ___ mg

.0001 kg = ___ g = ___ mg

.00001 kg = ___ g = ___ mg

(2) Find the equivalents for the following metric units for length.

1 m^2 = ___ cm^2 = ___ mm^2

$.001 \text{ m}^2$ = ___ cm^2 = ___ mm^2

$.000001 \text{ m}^2$ = ___ cm^2 = ___ mm^2

(3) Find the equivalents for the following metric units for volume.

1 L = ___ mL

.01 L = ___ mL

.001 L = ___ mL

Topic: The Metric System

Go to: *www.scilinks.org*

Code: ESS002

National Science Teachers Association

Part 2: (Student Lab Notebook Entries)

Anticipation Section Title: (A-2) Estimating With Metrics

Problem: Which equipment is best when measuring amounts of liquids? Of solids?

Prediction:

Note: Distribute the student handout (see *Part 3*) after students have completed their predictions.

Thinking About the Problem: Paraphrase the three main points of the reading in your own words.

(1)

(2)

(3)

Table 2.4. Data Table for Procedure #1: Estimating Mass

Object	Estimated Mass	Actual Mass
1		
2		
3		
4		
5		
6		
7		
8		
9		
10		

11		
12		
13		
14		
15		

Table 2.5. Data Table for Procedure #2: Estimating Dimensions

Object	Estimate	Actual
Your right arm (shoulder to finger tip)		
The classroom (north wall to south wall)		
A book (top to bottom edge)		
Your height (head to toe)		
A desk (surface to floor)		

Table 2.6. Data Table for Procedure #3: Estimating Temperatures

Subject	Estimate	Actual
Room temperature		
Hot tap water		
Cold tap water		

Table 2.7. Data Table for Procedure #4: Estimating Volume

Container	Volume Estimate	Volume Actual
Bucket of water		

Analysis:

(1) Which equipment should be used to measure liquids? Why?

(2) Which equipment should be used to measure solids? Why?

(3) Circle the most sensible measurement:

- Length of a football field: A) 90 mm; B) 90 cm; C) 90 m; D) 90 km

- Height of a woman: A) 160 mm; B) 160 cm; C) 160 m; D) 160 km

- Width of a room: A) 8 mm; B) 8 cm; C) 8 m; D) 8 km

- Width of a desk: A) 75 mm; B) 75 cm; C) 75 m: D) 75 km

- Mass of a dog: A) 8 mg; B) 8 g; C) 8 kg; D) 8 metric tons

- Mass of a pencil: A) 5 mg; B) 5 g; C) 5 kg; D) 5 metric tons

- Mass of a raisin: A) 1 mg; B) 1 g; C) 1 kg; D) 1 metric ton

- Mass of an adult: A) 60 mg; B) 60 g; C) 60 kg; D) 60 metric tons

- Volume of car gas tank: A) 8 mL; B) 8 L; C) 80 mL; D) 80 L

- Volume of a coffee cup: A) 250 mL; B) 250 L; C) 25 mL; D) 25 L

- Volume of a bathtub: A) 400 mL; B) 400 L; C) 40 mL; D) 40 L

- Volume of a pop can: A) 500 mL; B) 500 L; C) 5 mL; D) 5 L

- Temperature of boiling water: A) 100°C; B) 50°C; C) 212°C; D) 1000 °C

- Temperature of ice: A) 0°C; B) 32°C; C) 60°C; D) 100 °C

- Room temperature: A) 22°C; B) 55°C; C) 72°C; D) 100 °C

- Body temperature: A) 97°C; B) 37°C; C) 310°C; D) 100 °C

Concluding-the-Analysis Statements:

(1) I learned…

(2) If I were to re-do this lab, I would change…

(3) An example of a variable in this lab is…

(4) An example of a control in this lab is…

Part 3: (Student Handout)

Note: Distribute to students after they complete the Prediction in *Part 2*.

Anticipation Section Title: (A-2) Estimating With Metrics

Thinking About the Problem

Can you name any advantages of the metric system (*metricus*, "relating to measurement" in Latin)? Does it make any difference if we measure in yards and feet versus meters and centimeters? Today scientists collaborate with colleagues all over the world, and it is vital that they have similar tools and standards of measurement at their disposal.

Two of the most important process skills that scientists use every day are estimations of measurement and the manipulation of standard laboratory equipment. Without skill in these two areas, accurate observations would be impossible. This is especially true when it comes to modeling the vast distances found in the study of astronomy.

As you have witnessed in Lab A-1, knowledge of the metric system is vital in science. Background knowledge of the metric system lends a globally understood language to findings by scientists. Many scientists from across the world are responsible for discoveries in astronomy and need to communicate effectively for the findings to be widely understood. Most units of scientific measure are defined by universal constants. For example, one meter is defined as the distance traveled by light in a vacuum in $1/299,792,458$ of a second.

In this lab, you will enhance your skills in the areas of metric conversions, estimations of measurement, and the manipulation of standard laboratory equipment.

Data Collection Materials:

- Beakers

- Graduated cylinder

- Metric ruler

- Metric thermometer

- Triple beam balance

Data Collection Procedures:

(1) First estimate, the mass and then use the triple beam balance to measure the mass of 15 miscellaneous objects from around the room.

(2) Estimate the length of the following and then use a metric ruler to find the exact length: your arm, the room, a textbook, your height, and a desk.

(3) Estimate the temperature of the following and then use a metric thermometer to find the exact temperature: room temperature, hot tap water, and cold tap water.

(4) Estimate the volume of water in the bucket provided by your teacher. Then use a graduated cylinder to determine the exact volume.

Lab Astronomy 3: (A-3) Keeping Your Distance

Part 1: (Teacher's Lesson Plan Outline)

Note: See Lesson Planning on page 32.

Anticipation Section Title: (A-3) Keeping Your Distance

Problem: How far apart are the planets?

Prediction: Describe how big you think the solar system is, in terms of distance between the planets.

Thinking About the Problem: (See p. 54.)

Data Collection Materials and Procedures: (See p. 55.)

Teacher Directions for Data Collection Procedures Part 2:

(1) Put down the model Sun and start counting heel-to-toe steps.

(2) After 10 steps, mark the spot with Mercury's flag.

(3) After 9 more steps, mark the spot with Venus's.

(4) After 7 more steps, mark the spot with Earth's.

(5) After 14 more steps, mark the spot with Mar's.

(6) Take 55 steps, and mark the spot for Ceres's.

(7) Take 95 steps to Jupiter's.

(8) Take 112 steps to Saturn's.

(9) Take 249 steps to Uranus's.

(10) Take 281 steps to Neptune's.

(11) Take 242 more steps to Pluto's.

(12) It would take 399 more steps to get to Eris. If you would like to go to Proxima Centauri, the next nearest star beyond our Sun, it would 140 days of continuous steps.

Topic: Solar System

Go to: *www.scilinks.org*

Code: ESS003

Expansion and Further Investigation:

(1) Make an "Our Community Solar System Map." On a large map of our community, locate our middle school, and label it "Sun." Using a scale of 1AU = 1 cm, draw a circle representing each planet's orbit at the appropriate distance from the "Sun." Find and label your home to show which planet orbits nearest it.

(2) Approximately how many times farther from the Sun is Pluto than Earth? How about the dwarf planet Charon? How about the plutoid Eris? Describe the distances involved in the other objects found in the Kuiper Belt.

Part 2: (Student Lab Notebook Entries)

Anticipation Section Title: (A-3) Keeping Your Distance

Problem: How far apart are the planets?

Prediction:

Note: Distribute the student handout (see *Part 3*) after students have completed their predictions.

Thinking About the Problem: Paraphrase the three main points of the reading in your own words.

(1)

(2)

(3)

Table 2.8. Sketch for Procedure #4

Table 2.9. Data Collection Table #1: Distances Between the Sun and Planets

Planet Name	Average Distance (AU)
Classical Planets	
Mercury	0.38
Venus	0.72
Earth	1.00
Mars	1.52
Jupiter	5.20
Saturn	9.50
Uranus	19.20
Neptune	30.00
Plutoid Planets	
Pluto	39.50
Eris	97.00
Dwarf Planets	
Ceres	2.76
Charon	97.00

Analysis:

(1) Describe the trend, or pattern, found in the distance between planets as you move outward from the Sun.

(2) Combine what you've learned from both Lab A-1 and Lab A-2. What general statement can you make about how the size of a planet relates to its distance from the Sun?

(3) Describe in detail how big you think the solar system is.

Concluding-the-Analysis Statements:

(1) I learned…

(2) If I were to re-do this lab, I would change…

(3) An example of a variable in this lab is…

(4) An example of a control in this lab is…

Part 3: (Student Handout)

Note: Distribute to students after they complete the Prediction in *Part 2.*

Anticipation Section Title: (A-3) Keeping Your Distance

Thinking About the Problem

Have you ever thought about how big our solar system is? With all of the classical planets, the plutoid planets, the dwarf planets, the moons, and the many comets and asteroids you are learning about, it may seem pretty crowded. But space in the solar system is surprisingly empty. Planets (*planasthai*, "to wander" in Greek), which are the largest bodies orbiting the Sun, are tiny compared with the Sun itself.

The distances between the planets are immensely larger than the size of the planets themselves. You may already know that Earth orbits the Sun at an average distance of 150 million kilometers (93 million miles). This distance is called one astronomical unit, or 1 AU. But do you know how far Mars is from the Sun? Do you know how far Neptune is?

Beyond Neptune is a region of icy objects, some with very large diameters, orbiting the Sun in what is called the trans-Neptunian region. The innermost section of this far away region is the Kuiper belt, named after Dutch-American astronomer Gerard Kuiper. It is in this region where some plutoid planets, such as Pluto and Eris, and some dwarf planets, such as Charon, are found. It is also believed that this region could be the source for some comets, such as Comet Halley and Comet Encke. You will investigate comets further in Lab A-7.

In this two-part lab, you will see for yourself how widely separated the planets are. Although, we will use circles to illustrate the orbits of the planets, their actual orbits are elliptical (*elleipein*, "to fall short" in Greek). Elliptical orbits are slightly flattened circles.

Data Collection Materials:

- 1m x 1m butcher paper
- Calculator
- Cardboard square
- Drawing compass
- Long stretch of straight land outside
- Metric ruler
- Model Sun
- Pushpin
- Scissors
- Sewing thread
- Ten small landscape flags

Data Collection Procedures:

(1) Use the ruler to find the center of your butcher paper. Draw a small dot in the center, labeling it "Sun."

(2) Refer to Data Collection Table #1 for the orbit distance in centimeters (Use the scale of 1AU = 1 cm). For the first five planets, use the drawing compass to make circles of the proper radius on the paper. Label each planet.

(3) For the other planets, including the plutoid planet Pluto, you will draw the orbits using thread as a compass. Stop when you reach the edge of the paper.

(4) Draw and label a sketch of the planets and the Sun, showing approximate distances. Your sketch should indicate patterns in the spaces between planets.

(5) Take a walk through the solar system with your teacher.

Lab Astronomy 4: (A-4) Comparing Planetary Compounds

Part 1: (Teacher's Lesson Plan Outline)

Note: See Lesson Planning on page 32.

Anticipation Section Title: (A-4) Comparing Planetary Compounds

Problem: How are the planets closer to the Sun different from the planets that are farther away?

Prediction: Describe, in one sentence, how you think the planets differ from one another.

Thinking About the Problem: (See p. 61.)

Data Collection Materials and Procedures: (See p. 62.)

Safety Requirements: goggles, aprons

Note: In procedure 1 (p. 62), teachers should discuss the concept of *meniscus*, perhaps showing a diagram of this adhesion-in-a-cylinder event through the use of a transparency. Reading the volume from the bottom of the meniscus enables the students to be more accurate.

Expansion and Further Investigation:

(1) Use resources to find the density of the Earth's Moon. Add it to Data Collection Table #2, and see what the Moon might be made of. Find the density of Pluto, as well, to see what it might be made of.

(2) Using the procedure described in Part A, measure the density of five other materials. Create a data table similar to Data Collection Table #1 to report your findings.

(3) Use resources to investigate the composition of each of the planets and the larger moons in greater detail. Note that liquid water (required for life) has a density similar to, but slightly higher than, ice. Based on your findings, speculate on what other objects in the Solar System might support life.

_SCI_LINKS.
THE WORLD'S A CLICK AWAY

Topic: Inner Planets

Go to: _www.scilinks.org_

Code: ESS004

_SCI_LINKS.
THE WORLD'S A CLICK AWAY

Topic: Outer Planets

Go to: _www.scilinks.org_

Code: ESS005

Part 2: (Student Lab Notebook Entries)

Anticipation Section Title: (A-4) Comparing Planetary Compounds

Problem: How are the planets closer to the Sun different from the planets that are farther away?

Prediction:

Note: Distribute the student handout (see *Part 3*) after students have completed their predictions.

Thinking About the Problem: Paraphrase the three main points of the reading in your own words.

(1)

(2)

(3)

Table 2.10. Data Collection Table #1: Densities of Planet Components

Object	Rock	Iron	Ice
Mass (g)			
Starting Water Volume (mL)			
Ending Water Volume (mL)			
Change in Volume (mL)			
Density (g/mL)			

Table 2.11. Data Collection Table #2: Density Comparison (g/mL)

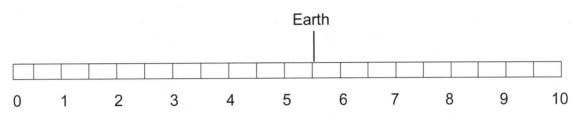

Table 2.12. Data Collection Table #3: Known Densities of Planets

Classical Planet	Density (g/mL)
Mercury	5.43
Venus	5.24
Earth	5.52
Mars	3.93
Jupiter	1.33
Saturn	0.69
Uranus	1.32
Neptune	1.64

Analysis:

(1) List rock, iron, and ice in order of increasing density.

(2) Given a sample of unknown material, describe one way you might determine if it is more similar to rock, iron, or ice.

(3) Looking at Data Collection Table #2, determine the two main types of material (rock, iron, or ice) that compose each of the planets listed below. (In reality, "ice" on planets might take the form of compressed gases, like methane.)

Mercury =

Venus =

Earth =

Mars =

Jupiter =

Saturn =

Uranus =

Neptune =

Concluding-the-Analysis Statements:

(1) I learned…

(2) If I were to re-do this lab, I would change…

(3) An example of a variable in this lab is…

(4) An example of a control in this lab is…

Part 3: (Student Handout)

Note: Distribute to students after they complete the Prediction in *Part 2*.

Anticipation Section Title: (A-4) Comparing Planetary Compounds

---

Thinking About the Problem

What are the planets made of? Isn't the firm ground we stand on basically the same as it would be on any of the other planets? Well, there are some planets that we would have a very hard time "standing" on, because they are composed basically of compressed gases and ice, and their vast size makes their gravitational pulls far too strong for human legs to withstand. These include the biggest of the planets in our solar system: Jupiter, Neptune, Saturn, and Uranus.

Made up mainly of lighter compounds, such as methane and hydrogen, the *Gas Giant* planets are only really solid at their cores. Conversely, the four planets that are closest to the Sun—Earth, Mars, Mercury, and Venus—are solid both at their cores and at their crusts. Because they each have a surface that is hard, they are grouped together as the *Terrestrial* planets (*terra,* "Earth" in Latin, *terre* in French, *tierra* in Spanish). The basic composition of Earth's core is iron, but there are also significant amounts of nickel and sulfur.

The compositions of the planets is dictated in part by their distances from the Sun. Separating the Gas Giants from the Terrestrial planets is a frost line, located 3.4 AU from the Sun, in the main asteroid belt. Inside the frost line, temperatures are high enough that only metallic elements are able to condense into solids. Beyond the frost line, temperatures are cool enough to allow even hydrogen and helium to condense into ices. By comparing the Gas Giants and the Terrestrial planets we can gain insight into the formation of our solar system.

At its start, our solar system was formed with a young star, which we call Sun, plus a considerable amount of matter, within the Sun's gravitational reach, including very hot metals and gasses. As time went by, this matter cooled, and rocks and metals that were closer to the Sun condensed into solids, while gasses did not. In the outermost planets, however, the light compounds as well as the rocks and metals condensed into types of ice. On the Terrestrial planets, light compounds such as hydrogen and methane remained as gasses; on the Gas Giant planets, being much farther from the Sun's warmth, even these light compounds often condensed into solid form.

As a result of their relative distances from the Sun, the planets Earth, Mars, Mercury, and Venus are composed mainly of metal and rock and are therefore smaller than the larger planets that contain a lot of ice and gas in addition to their solid cores. In this two-part lab, you will investigate densities of ice, stone, and iron, to learn about the composition of the planets.

Data Collection Materials:

- 2 steel bolts (made of iron)

- 250 mL graduated cylinder

- Ice cubes

- Metric ruler

- Obsidian rock

- Triple beam balance

Data Collection Procedures:

(1) Fill the graduated cylinder with about 100 mL of water. Read the exact volume and record this value as the "starting water volume" in Data Collection Table #1.

(2) Measure the mass of the rock in grams. Record results in Data Collection Table #1.

(3) As soon as you have measured the rock's mass, place it into the graduated cylinder. Read the "ending water volume" and record it in Data Collection Table #1.

(4) Subtract the starting water volume from the ending water volume, entering the result as "change in volume" in Data Collection Table #1.

(5) Remember that density equals mass divided by volume. Use the following equation to calculate the density of the rock:

Mass of Object (g) ÷ Change in Volume (mL) = Density (g/mL).

(6) Repeat step #1–#5, using the iron and then the ice. When working with the ice, work quickly. Since it floats, use the tip of your pencil to push it down so that it is just barely submerged. Record your results in Data Collection Table #1.

(7) Use the data from Data Collection Table #1, to make a vertical line 2 cm high for rock, iron, and ice on Data Collection Table #2.

(8) Make a vertical line 1 cm high on Data Collection Table #2 for each of the planets listed in Data Collection Table #3. Label the lines for each planet. Earth has been done for you.

Lab Astronomy 5: (A-5) Reflecting on the Solar System

Part 1: (Teacher's Lesson Plan Outline)

Note: See Lesson Planning on page 32.

Anticipation Section Title: (A-5) Reflecting on the Solar System

Problem: Can the amount of reflected light teach us about a distant planet?

Prediction: Describe, in one sentence, what materials you would use to build a small object that would increase in temperature when placed in direct sunlight.

Thinking About the Problem: (See p. 70.)

Data Collection Materials and Procedures: (See p. 71.)

Note: Low albedo devices (LADs) can be as simple as a shoebox painted black or a dark metal cooking pan with plastic wrap covering its top.

Note: In procedure 1, teachers should discuss the concept of *meniscus*, perhaps showing a diagram of this adhesion-in-a-cylinder event through the use of a diagram. Reading the volume from the bottom of the meniscus enables the students to be more accurate.

Expansion and Further Investigation:

(1) The albedo of Earth is such a critical factor in understanding climate and global warming that it has become a very important quantity to measure. Use resources to learn about specifics on Earth's albedo. Using a map of the world, describe specifically how the albedo changes as you move around the surface of the Earth. Include all necessary details.

(2) In one half page, describe specifically how the Earth's albedo changes with the seasons. Include all necessary details.

(3) Use the information from Data Collection Table #1 to make a graph of temperature versus time. Find an equation that describes the line generated by this data.

SCi*LINKS*
THE WORLD'S A CLICK AWAY

Topic: Albedo

Go to: *www.scilinks.org*

Code: ESS006

Part 2: (Student Lab Notebook Entries)

Anticipation Section Title: (A-5) Reflecting on the Solar System

Problem: Can the amount of reflected light teach us about a distant planet?

Prediction:

Note: Distribute the student handout (see *Part 3*) after students have completed their predictions.

Thinking About the Problem: Paraphrase the three main points of the reading in your own words.

(1)

(2)

(3)

Table 2.13. Sketch for Procedure #2

Table 2.14. Data Collection Table #1: Time Versus Temperature for LAD

Time (min.)	Temperature (°C)	Time (min.)	Temperature (°C)
0.0		10.0	
0.5		10.5	
1.0		11.0	
1.5		11.5	
2.0		12.0	
2.5		12.5	
3.0		13.0	
3.5		13.5	
4.0		14.0	
4.5		14.5	
5.0		15.0	
5.5		15.5	
6.0		16.0	
6.5		16.5	
7.0		17.0	
7.5		17.5	
8.0		18.0	
8.5		18.5	
9.0		19.0	
9.5		19.5	
		20.0	

Table 2.15. Data Collection Table #2: Albedos of Solar System Objects

Object	Type of Object	Albedo
Mercury	Planet	0.06
Venus	Planet	0.76
Earth	Planet	0.40 (average)
Moon	Moon of Earth	0.07
Mars	Planet	0.16
Phobos	Moon of Mars	0.018
Ceres	Dwarf planet (former asteroid)	0.11
Vesta	Asteroid	0.38
Jupiter	Planet	0.51
Europa	Moon of Jupiter	0.60
Callisto	Moon of Jupiter	0.20
Saturn	Planet	0.50
Titan	Moon of Saturn	0.20
Uranus	Planet	0.66
Oberon	Moon of Uranus	0.05
Neptune	Planet	0.62
Triton	Moon of Neptune	0.80
Pluto	Plutoid planet (trans-Neptunian object)	0.50
Charon	Dwarf planet (former moon of Pluto)	0.37
Eris	Plutoid planet (trans-Neptunian object)	0.75

Table 2.16. Data Collection Table #3: Planetary Albedos With
Gray Scale Chart

Gray Scale Chart	Albedo	Solar System Objects
	0.00 – 0.10	
	0.11 – 0.30	
	0.31 – 0.45	
	0.46 – 0.55	
	0.56 – 0.85	
	0.86 – 1.00	

Analysis:

(1) Give a working definition of *albedo*.

(2) Compare your LAD with your classmates' LADs. Which method worked best for reflecting the least light energy? Explain.

(3) Determine, using the Gray Scale Chart, what the average albedo is for your LAD.

(4) Which solar system object in Data Collection Table #2 has the highest albedo? Which has the lowest albedo?

(5) Is the albedo of the Earth's Moon more like that of a snowball or a lump of charcoal?

(6) Describe, in detail, the changes in temperature of your LAD during the 20 minutes in the sun.

(7) How did the albedo of your device influence what happened during the 20 minutes in the sun?

Concluding-the-Analysis Statements:

(1) I learned…

(2) If I were to re-do this lab, I would change…

(3) An example of a variable in this lab is…

(4) An example of a control in this lab is…

Part 3: (Student Handout)

Note: Distribute to students after they complete the Prediction in *Part 2*.

Anticipation Section Title: (A-5) Reflecting on the Solar System

Thinking About the Problem

Have you ever looked up at the Moon on a cloudless night? The Moon seems so bright; you might imagine it to be covered in something highly reflective like snow or bright yellow paint. But looks are deceiving. In fact, if you held a piece of the lunar surface (*luna*, "moon" in Latin and Spanish, *lune* in French) in your hand it would appear very dark. The Moon only appears bright in the sky because it is illuminated by a tremendous amount of light from the Sun. It reflects some of that light back out into space, enabling you to see it so clearly.

The fraction of the light falling on a solar system object that is then reflected back into space is called its "albedo." The albedo (*albus*, "white" in Latin) of an object can range from nearly zero (no light reflected back) to almost one (all light reflected back).

Observing the albedo of an object can help us determine what materials make up the object. A low albedo probably indicates a surface composed of dark rocks, as on the Moon. A high albedo is often due to the presence of clouds, as on Venus, or of a frozen icy surface, as on Neptune.

Earth's albedo is less predictable because of large variations in cloud cover. The wide variation in Earth's albedo is an important factor in studies of long-term climate and global warming. Any light energy that does penetrate the clouds gets trapped below them, a condition called the "greenhouse effect."

A low albedo means that much of the incoming light and heat energy from the Sun is absorbed. The object that absorbs most of this energy will be warmer than an object that reflects away most of its light energy.

Data Collection Materials:

- Metric thermometer

- Various household objects used to build your low albedo device

Data Collection Procedures:

(1) Build a low albedo device (LAD) out of simple materials. It will be due: _____.

(2) Examine your LAD. Make mental observations about its size, color, and construction materials. Draw a labeled sketch of your LAD.

(3) Magnifying glasses (and heat sources) will not be allowed and your device must hold one metric thermometer.

(4) Record the temperature (in degrees Celsius) versus time (in minutes) results of your LAD investigation for 20 minutes in Data Collection Table #1.

(5) Use the information in Data Collection Table #2 to organize and compare the albedos of various solar system objects in Data Collection Table #3.

Lab Astronomy 6: (A-6) Landing on the Moon

Part 1: (Teacher's Lesson Plan Outline)

Note: See Lesson Planning on page 32.

Anticipation Section Title: (A-6) Landing on the Moon

Problem: How would the differences between environments on the Moon and on Earth affect your survival?

Prediction: Describe two ways in which your life would be different if you lived on the Moon.

Thinking About the Problem: (See p. 76.)

Data Collection Materials and Procedures: (See p. 77.)

Note: Many insights for students can be gained by using an outside reading reference about the Moon's environment after this lab. References can be found in textbooks, media centers, and online. Students will be fascinated to learn that the lack of atmosphere prevents the lighting of any match. The lack of magnetic poles prevents the proper functioning of a compass. Travel on the moon will be affected by the fact that the pull of gravity is only one-sixth that of the Earth. And the lack of water makes several of the items listed on page 77 useless.

Expansion and Further Investigation:

(1) Do the Tic-Tac-Know (see Appendix B) differentiation assignment, demonstrating your results to the class.

(2) Research and explain to the class how Earth's Moon is similar to, and different from, the moons of the planet Jupiter.

(3) What do scientists believe led to the formation of our Moon? What evidence do they use to back up their hypotheses? Draw several labeled diagrams to show what you learned.

SC*LINKS*
THE WORLD'S A CLICK AWAY

Topic: Earth's Moon

Go to: *www.scilinks.org*

Code: ESS007

Part 2: (Student Lab Notebook Entries)

Anticipation Section Title: (A-6) Landing on the Moon

Problem: How would the differences between environments on the Moon and on Earth affect your survival?

Prediction:

Note: Distribute the student handout (see *Part 3*) after students have completed their predictions.

Thinking About the Problem: Paraphrase the three main points of the reading in your own words.

(1)

(2)

(3)

Table 2.17. Data Collection Table #1

Item Name (in order of priority)	Justification Statement
(1)	
(2)	
(3)	
(4)	
(5)	
(6)	
(7)	

(8)	
(9)	
(10)	
(11)	
(12)	
(13)	
(14)	
(15)	
(16)	
(17)	
(18)	
(19)	
(20)	
(21)	

Analysis:

(1) Which three items would be the most valuable on the Moon during an emergency? Explain why.

(2) Give an example of each of three ways in which your life would be different on the Moon.

(3) What specific things will you look for in determining whether you could live on other planets in our solar system?

Concluding-the-Analysis Statements:

(1) I learned…

(2) If I were to re-do this lab, I would change…

(3) An example of a variable in this lab is…

(4) An example of a control in this lab is…

Part 3: (Student Handout)

Note: Distribute to students after they complete the Prediction in *Part 2*.

Anticipation Section Title: (A-6) Landing on the Moon

Thinking About the Problem

Have you ever thought about going to the Moon? This lab involves problem-solving in a simulated landing on the Moon.

Imagine that you are an astronaut and you are a member of a crew traveling to the Moon. Your spaceship is part of a convoy and each ship has its own crew (a group of your classmates). The convoy, unfortunately, is forced to land a considerable distance from the lunar base, and because the landing area is rough, all the ships receive minor damage during landing. None of the crewmembers is seriously hurt, but because the spaceship is disabled and the radios are broken, there is no way to signal for help. The travel distance from the crash point to the nearest base is 50 km. Each crew must get to the base without outside help.

Your main task in this activity is to decide which emergency supplies to take with you. Only the background knowledge of your fellow crewmembers can be used to help you make choices. No outside resources can be used, yet.

Data Collection Materials:

- Compass
- Extra oxygen
- First aid kit
- Flashlight
- Freeze-dried food
- Fuel for stove
- Inflatable raft
- Map of Moon
- Matches
- Mirror
- Parachute

- Pressure suits
- Raincoats
- Signal flares
- Sleeping bags
- Small stove
- Standard tent
- Suit repair kit
- Ten meters of rope
- Torches
- Water

Data Collection Procedures:

(1) As a lab group you must discuss the importance or usefulness of each item.

(2) Each group member must make a list of the items, in order of priority, on his/her lab report.

(3) Each group member must write a statement next to each item, which justifies why he/she ranked the item in that position.

Lab Astronomy 7: (A-7) Orbiting Snowballs

Part 1: (Teacher's Lesson Plan Outline)

Note: See Lesson Planning on page 32.

Anticipation Section Title: (A-7) Orbiting Snowballs

Problem: How are comets similar to, and different from, snowballs?

Prediction: Describe, in one sentence, the answer to the problem statement.

Thinking About the Problem: (See p. 81.)

Data Collection Materials and Procedures: (See pp. 82–83.)

Safety Requirements: goggles, aprons, protective gloves

SCI LINKS.
THE WORLD'S A CLICK AWAY

Topic: Comets
Go to: *www.scilinks.org*
Code: ESS008

Expansion and Further Investigation:

(1) Imagine yourself as Earth, orbiting the Sun in a circle inside a comet's orbit. Describe the relative positions of the Earth, Sun, and comet that yield the best visibility from Earth. Do the same for worst visibility.

(2) Disaster movies have been made about the impact of a comet or asteroid on Earth. We have never seen such an impact on Earth firsthand, but in 1994, Comet Shoemaker-Levy 9 collided with Jupiter and was observed by the Hubble Space Telescope. Use the internet to learn about this impact. Write a detailed half-page report on this incident.

Part 2: (Student Lab Notebook Entries)

Anticipation Section Title: (A-7) Orbiting Snowballs

Problem: How are comets similar to, and different from, snowballs?

Prediction:

Note: Distribute the student handout (see *Part 3*) after students have completed their predictions.

Thinking About the Problem: Paraphrase the three main points of the reading in your own words.

   (1)

   (2)

   (3)

Table 2.18. Sketch for Data Collection Procedure #7

Table 2.19. Data Collection Table #1: Comet Changes

Time (min.)	Observations of Comet	Description of Change
1		
5		
10		
15		
20		

Analysis:

(1) Summarize your observations of the comet during the course of the 20 minutes.

(2) How did the appearance of the comet change from the beginning of the investigation to the end?

(3) Use the Thinking About the Problem section to help you describe what happens to a comet as it approaches the Sun.

(4) Why is a comet sometimes said to be similar to a "dirty snowball"?

Concluding-the-Analysis Statements:

(1) I learned…

(2) If I were to re-do this lab, I would change…

(3) An example of a variable in this lab is…

(4) An example of a control in this lab is…

Part 3: (Student Handout)

Note: Distribute to students after they complete the Prediction in *Part 2.*

Anticipation Section Title: (A-7) Orbiting Snowballs

Thinking About the Problem

Have you ever made a snowball that started falling apart as soon as you threw it? Temperature, moisture levels, and debris within the snow all play a role in allowing the snowball to remain compacted when you throw it. That analogy may help in our study of comets during this lab.

The stars in the night sky seem unchanging. The constellations your parents and grandparents knew are the same ones you can see tonight. The stable orbits of the planets carry them around the sky in predictable ways. Everything is orderly. But once in a while, something spectacular appears. A comet (*kome*, "hair," and *aster*, "star," in Greek) is a leftover remnant of the early formation of the solar system. It blazes in the sky for a few weeks as it passes through our section of the solar system.

In relatively recent years there have been some spectacular comets, easily visible with the naked eye. There were, for example, Comet Halley in 1986, Comet Hyakutake in 1995, and Comet Hale-Bopp in 1996. Extending outward from the bright head of the comet, the magnificent tail can stretch halfway across the sky. No wonder comets have been regarded with fear, awe, and suspicion throughout history.

Far from the Sun, a comet is dark. It has only a small "nucleus" (2–3 km diameter) made up of an icy sphere mixed with rock and dust. The frozen gases in the ice include water, carbon dioxide, ammonia, and some organic compounds. As comet approaches the Sun, the "coma" and the "tail" begin to develop (see Illustration 2.1). The Sun's radiation heats the ices on the nucleus, but they don't melt directly into liquid. Instead of melting, the ices "sublime" directly from a solid to a gas. Light from the Sun then reflects off of these gases, making them appear to glow.

Some of the glowing gas forms the "coma," which surrounds and hides the nucleus. The rest of the gas streams back behind the comet (always in a direction away from the Sun) forming the "tail." As the ices sublime, some of the dust and broken pieces of rock mix in, adding to the length of the tail. Comet tails can stretch for many millions of kilometers across space.

Illustration 2.1. Comet

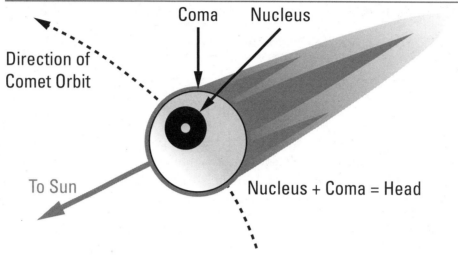

Data Collection Materials:

- Carbonated dark cola (15 mL)

- Dry ice (1 kg)

- Hammer

- Newspaper

- Protective gloves (worn always)

- Soil (10 g)

- Three resealable plastic sandwich bags

- Water (200 mL)

Data Collection Procedures:

(1) Each lab group should place the set of plastic bags inside another to form a triple-layer bag.

(2) Place the dry ice in the bag, carefully crumbling it with the hammer.

(3) Hold bag while your partner adds dirt and cola.

(4) Squeeze the bottom of the bag to mix the ingredients evenly.

(5) Add the water. Immediately begin packing the materials inside the bag into a snowball shape.

(6) Remove the comet from the bag and place it on the newspaper.

(7) Observe and record the changes that your comet undergoes for 20 minutes. Draw and label a sketch of your comet.

Lab Astronomy 8: (A-8) Hunting for Space Flight History

Part 1: (Teacher's Lesson Plan Outline)

Note: See Lesson Planning on page 32.

Anticipation Section Title: (A-8) Hunting for Space Flight History

Problem: What does a paper clip have to do with space travel?

Prediction: Describe, in one sentence, your answer to the problem statement.

Thinking About the Problem: (See p. 88.)

Data Collection Materials and Procedures: (See p. 88.)

Table 2.20. Notes for Teacher on Symbolism

Object	Symbolism in Space Flight History
"8"	Apollo 8 became the first manned mission to orbit the Moon in 1968.
Australia	Most of Skylab's parts fell over Australia, when it de-orbited in 1979.
Belt	The U.S. launched its first artificial satellite, Explorer I, in January 1958. It discovered the Van Allen Radiation Belt around the Earth.
Cough drop	The first crew to catch colds in space was on Apollo 7 in 1968.
Diaper	Alan Shepard was America's first astronaut in April 1961. Due to his wetting himself while he was waiting to be launched, all future astronauts would wear urine collection devices (diapers).
Eagle **	Neil Armstrong and Buzz Aldrin became the first people to land and walk on the Moon on July 20, 1969, in Apollo 11, nicknamed the Eagle.
Hornet	A quarantine facility aboard an aircraft carrier named the Hornet was a brief home to the first three Apollo lunar landing missions (1969–1970).

Joystick	Lunar rovers, controlled by joysticks, were used to drive on the Moon during the Apollo 15, 16, and 17 (1970–1971) missions.
Lemon	Gus Grissom hung a lemon on the Apollo 1 capsule, signifying that he thought it was a piece of junk. He was correct. He and two other crewmembers died in it during a practice launch on January 27, 1967.
Liberty Bell **	In 1961, Gus Grissom had a mechanical malfunction upon landing his Liberty Bell 7 capsule in the ocean. He almost drowned.
Monkey **	Three monkeys, Gordo, Able, and Baker, were launched into space on separate missions in 1959.
Ohio State quarter	John Glenn, featured on the Ohio State quarter, became the first American to orbit the Earth in 1962.
Paper Clip	100 German rocket scientists, at the end of World War II in 1945, were brought to the United States under the code name Operation Paper Clip.
Rock	Harrison Schmitt, the first geologist, collected Moon rocks while on Apollo 17 (1971).
Spider **	Arabella, a spider, proved that spiders could spin a web in space in 1973 on the first U.S. space station, Skylab.
Sweatband	Eugene Cernan's space walk had to be cut short due to profuse sweating on Gemini 9, in 1966.
Tether	Ed White performed the first space walk, held by a tethered air line to Gemini 4 in 1965.
Thermometer	The world's first artificial satellite was launched by the Soviet Union in 1957. It was named Sputnik, and its job was to collect data on atmospheric temperatures.
Tom Hanks **	Tom Hanks was in the movie *Apollo 13*. That mission had to be canceled in 1970 due to an oxygen tank explosion.
Two magnets	Magnets enabled the first docking in space in 1966 between Gemini 8 and a satellite.

Note: ** Denotes the five easiest symbols to connect to space flight history. This may be helpful for special-needs adaptations in inclusion classes.

Expansion and Further Investigation:

(1) Research Russian space history events. Describe, in a detailed half-page report, how Russian space history inspired and paralleled that of the United States.

(2) Research Canadian space flight history events, especially the important contributions to the International Space Station. Report your findings to the class.

(3) Research animal space flight history. Create a time line, listing the various events that involved animals from many nations.

(4) Develop a list of five recent symbols, with brief explanations, that tie into global space flight history (1980 to present day).

SCILINKS.
THE WORLD'S A CLICK AWAY

Topic: How Have People Explored Space?

Go to: *www.scilinks.org*

Code: ESS009

Part 2: (Student Lab Notebook Entries)

Anticipation Section Title: (A-8) Hunting for Space Flight History

Problem: What does a paper clip have to do with space travel?

Prediction:

Note: Distribute the student handout (see *Part 3*) after students have completed their predictions.

Thinking About the Problem: Paraphrase the three main points of the reading in your own words.

(1)

(2)

(3)

Table 2.21. Data Collection Table #1: Student Explanations of Symbolism

Object	Symbolism in Space Flight History
"8"	
Australia	
Belt	
Cough drop	
Diaper	
Eagle	
Hornet	
Joystick	
Lemon	
Liberty Bell	
Monkey	
Ohio State quarter	
Paper Clip	

Rock	
Spider	
Sweatband	
Tether	
Thermometer	
Tom Hanks	
Two magnets	

Analysis:

(1) In your teams, create a time line of space history events, using the notes from our scavenger hunt.

(2) Make a list of the three websites that gave you the best information for this scavenger hunt.

(3) Create a crossword puzzle, using information you learned about space flight history. Include five "across" clues, five "down" clues, and an answer key.

Concluding-the-Analysis Statements:

(1) I learned…

(2) If I were to re-do this lab, I would change…

(3) An example of a variable in this lab is…

(4) An example of a control in this lab is…

Part 3: (Student Handout)

Note: Distribute to students after they complete the Prediction in *Part 2*.

Anticipation Section Title: (A-8) Hunting for Space Flight History

---

Thinking About the Problem

Have you ever been part of a team on a scavenger hunt? Thanks to this lesson plan, with symbols borrowed from NASA, you are invited to participate on a hunt in (cyber) space. In some way, each of the objects in this scavenger hunt relates to a space flight history event that occurred between 1945 and 1979. Your task is to determine how each object is symbolic of something that happened in space flight history.

You and your group may use classroom computers (with internet connections) as a resource. You will have two class periods with computers to determine how each object relates to space flight history. This search can be very challenging, so use each of your group members for helpful advice during your searches.

At the end of our computer lab time, your group will compile its findings and hand them in to your teacher. We will then have a discussion about what aspect of space flight each object represents.

Data Collection Materials:

- Computers with internet access

- List of 20 scavenger hunt items (4 lists with 5 items on each, 1 per group)

Data Collection Procedures:

(1) Sit side by side with your group members in front of a computer.

(2) Review your list of objects. Use the internet to begin hunting for connections between the listed items and space flight history (1945–1979).

(3) Record the results of your search in Table 2.21. Data Collection Table #1.

Chapter 3

Geology

*N*ote to the teacher: In the geology unit, students become familiar with the chemical elements that make up minerals and rocks. They will understand that matter is made up of small particles, which can undergo physical and chemical changes, and this explains the properties of matter.

Students perform activities that introduce them to the difference between rocks and minerals. They also examine the various processes and interactions of the rock cycle. Students investigate a variety of geologic features and events on or near Earth's surface to develop an understanding of Earth's composition and structure. They observe that the rocks and minerals around us today are products of complex geologic processes. The students will also interpret successive layers of sedimentary rocks and their fossils to document the age and history of the Earth.

The 10-day outline in Table 3.1 assumes that your course started with the Earth Science Pretest, Lab S-1, and the astronomy unit. If, however, you choose to cover Geology first, we recommend that you still begin with the Pretest and Lab S-1 (see Chapter 1, "The First Ten Days").

Table 3.1. Possible Syllabus for the First Ten Days of Geology

Week 1	Day 1	Day 2	Day 3	Day 4	Day 5
	KWL flip book, Lab G-1 (anticipation)	Lab G-1 (begin data collection), "Edible Stalactites and Stalagmites" assigned	Lab G-1 (finish data collection and analysis)	Vocabulary of Geology notes, introduce the periodic table of elements, begin "Periodic Puns"	Lab G-1 (report due), "Periodic Puns" classroom work time
Week 2	Day 1	Day 2	Day 3	Day 4	Day 5
	Lab G-2 (anticipation)	Lab G-2 (data collection)	Lab G-2 (complete data collection and analysis)	"Periodic Puns" due, Lab G-3 (anticipation)	Lab G-3 (data collection), Lab G-2 (report due)

Lab Geology 1: (G-1) Weighing In on Minerals

Part 1: (Teacher's Lesson Plan Outline)

Note: See Lesson Planning on page 32.

Anticipation Section Title: (G-1) Weighing In on Minerals

Problem: What methods can geologists use to identify different minerals?

Prediction: Describe how knowing the density of a stone can help you identify it.

Thinking About the Problem: (See p. 95.)

Data Collection Materials and Procedures: (See p. 96.)

Safety Requirements: goggles, aprons

Note: **Key to mineral samples:** Minerals are calcite 2.7, halite 2.2, gypsum 2.3, feldspar 2.55, quartz 2.6, and magnetite 5.0.

Expansion and Further Investigation:

Topic: Identifying Minerals

Go to: *www.scilinks.org*

Code: ESS010

(1) Determine the density of three regularly shaped objects (wood block, for example) using both of the volume determination methods. Account for any differences you find.

(2) Design and perform an experiment to determine the year in which the composition of pennies was changed from copper to zinc. (The change occurred before 1993.)

(3) Assume you have an unknown liquid with a density of 3.0 g/mL; list all of the minerals that would float in that liquid.

Part 2: (Student Lab Notebook Entries)

Anticipation Section Title: (G-1) Weighing In on Minerals

Problem: What methods can geologists use to identify different minerals?

Prediction:

Note: Distribute the student handout (see *Part 3*) after students have completed their predictions.

Thinking About the Problem: Paraphrase the three main points of the reading in your own words.

   (1)

   (2)

   (3)

Table 3.2. Data Collection Table #1: Density of Minerals (Small Group)

Mineral	Mass (g)	Volume (mL)	Density (g/mL)
1			
2			
3			
4			
5			
6			

Table 3.3. Data Collection Table #2: Density of Minerals (Class Average)

Mineral	Group Results on Density of Each Mineral (g/mL)							Average Density (g/mL)
	Group A Results	Group B Results	Group C Results	Group D Results	Group E Results	Group F Results	Group G Results	
1								
2								
3								
4								
5								
6								

Analysis:

(1) If you were given a ring, how could you determine whether it was pure gold?

(2) Explain a method that you could use to determine your own body's density.

(3) If halite has a known density of 2.2, which of your minerals is most likely halite?

(4) If quartz has a known density of 2.6, which of your minerals is most likely quartz?

(5) If calcite has a known density of 2.7, which of your minerals is most likely calcite?

(6) If magnetite has a known density of 5.0, which of your minerals is most likely magnetite?

(7) If feldspar has a known density of 2.55, which of your minerals is most likely feldspar?

(8) If gypsum has a known desnity of 2.3., which of your minerals is most likely gypsum? (Hint: See Thinking About the Problem.)

Concluding-the-Analysis Statements:

(1) I learned…

(2) If I were to re-do this lab, I would change…

(3) An example of a variable in this lab is…

(4) An example of a control in this lab is…

Part 3: (Student Handout)

Note: Distribute to students after they complete the Prediction in *Part 2.*

Anticipation Section Title: (G-1) Weighing In on Minerals

Thinking About the Problem

How can scientists figure out which mineral they are examining? Minerals are Earth materials that have four main characteristics: They are solid, inorganic (not a mixture of carbon, hydrogen, and oxygen), and naturally occurring, and they have a definite chemical structure. Minerals are identifiable based on a number of different properties. One is the mineral's particular crystal structure. For example, quartz has a hexagonal (*hexa*, "six" in Greek) crystal form. One is the planes, or cleavage lines, along which a mineral is weakest and tends to fracture easily. Another is the luster, or the way that light tends to reflect off a mineral's surface. Still another is the color left behind, called streak, when a mineral scratches a porcelain surface.

Scientists use these methods to identify minerals. In this geology (*geo*, "earth" in Greek) unit, you will learn about two diagnostic tests for minerals: density (in Lab G-1) and hardness (in Lab G-2).

How can you tell how dense rocks and minerals are? Geologists have developed tools that help measure density. A triple beam balance is used for this purpose. In addition, if the mineral to be measured is a regularly shaped object, such as a cube, its volume can be determined with a mathematical formula, L x W x H, where the letters represent length, width, and height.

To measure the volume of objects that do not have a regular shape, the mathematical formula given above for volume does not work. In those cases, a water displacement method can be used. Density (often referred to as "specific gravity" in geology) determines the mass of the mineral in relation to the mass of an equal volume of water. Mineral densities can range from 1 to 20. For example, quartz has a density of 2.65 and is 2.65 times as heavy as the same volume of water. Density values under 2 for minerals are regarded as *light* (amber is 1.0). *Normal* is the term given to minerals with density values from 2 to 3 (calcite is 2.7). All minerals above 3.0 are considered *heavy* (galena is 7.4). Testing for density is how people determined if they had found gold during the Gold Rush in early American history.

Data Collection Materials:

- Graduated cylinder

- Six unknown mineral samples

- Triple beam balance

- Water

Data Collection Procedures:

(1) Determine and record the mass of all six minerals.

(2) Use the water displacement method with the graduated cylinder to determine the volume of all six minerals.

(3) Determine the density of each object ($D = M / V$).

(4) Record your density results in the class average data table.

(5) Complete the Edible Stalactites and Stalagmites project (see Appendix B), presenting your results to the class.

Lab Geology 2: (G-2) Knowing Mohs

Part 1: (Teacher's Lesson Plan Outline)

Note: See Lesson Planning on page 32.

Anticipation Section Title: (G-2) Knowing Mohs

Problem: Why are diamonds considered the hardest known mineral?

Prediction: Give a working definition of *mineral*.

Thinking About the Problem: (See p. 101.)

Data Collection Materials and Procedures: (See p. 101.)

Note: Review the Vocabulary of Geology Notes (see Appendix B), prior to beginning this lab. Assign, and give class time for, Periodic Puns (see Appendix B), as well.

Safety Requirements: goggles

Note: **Key to mineral samples:** Minerals are calcite 3, halite 2.25, gypsum 2, feldspar 6, quartz 7, and magnetite 5.75.

Expansion and Further Investigation:

(1) Research the functional uses of each mineral studied in this lab.

(2) Find examples in your own community of weathering and/or erosion. Prepare a presentation, using digital photos, to share with the class.

Part 2: (Student Lab Notebook Entries)

Anticipation Section Title: (G-2) Knowing Mohs

Problem: Why are diamonds considered the hardest known mineral?

Prediction:

Note: Distribute the student handout (see *Part 3*) after students have completed their predictions.

Thinking About the Problem: Paraphrase the three main points of the reading in your own words.

    (1)

    (2)

    (3)

Table 3.4. Data Collection Table #1: Hardness Test Results

Mineral Sample #	Fingernail Test	Copper Plate Test	Iron Nail Test	Glass Plate Test	Hardness Value
1					
2					
3					
4					
5					
6					

Table 3.5. Data Collection Table #2: Mohs's Hardness Scale

Test Result	Hardness Estimate	
	"Yes"	"No"
Can it be scratched by your fingernail?	<2	>2
Can it be scratched by the copper plate?	<3	>3
Can it be scratched by the iron nail?	<5	>5
Can it scratch the glass plate?	<6	>6

Table 3.6. Data Collection Table #3: Mohs's Mineral Hardness Values

Hardness	Mineral	Scratch Test Results
1	Talc	Easily scratched by fingernail
1.5	Graphite	Easily scratched by fingernail
2	Gypsum	Scratched by fingernail
2.25	Halite	Scratched by fingernail
2.5	Muscovite	Scratched by fingernail
2.75	Biotite	Not quite scratched by copper plate
3	Calcite	Slightly scratched by copper plate
4	Fluorite	Easily scratched by iron nail
5	Apatite	Scratched by iron nail
5.5	Pyroxine	Scratched by iron nail
5.75	Magnetite	Slightly scratched by iron nail; might scratch glass plate
6	Feldspar	Slightly scratched by iron nail; scratches glass plate
6.5	Olivine	Scratches glass plate
7	Quartz	Scratches both iron nail and glass plate
8	Topaz	Scratches quartz
9	Corundum	Scratches topaz
10	Diamond	Hardest known mineral

Analysis:

(1) Which method should you use to identify a mineral most accurately: its hardness value, appearance, or density? Explain.

(2) Imagine you have a mineral with a Mohs's scale of 2. Describe the procedure for determining this hardness value.

(3) Imagine you have a mineral with a Mohs's scale of 6. Describe the procedure for determining this hardness value.

(4) Describe the relationship between a mineral's hardness and its ability to be worn away by the processes of either weathering or erosion.

(5) Use the Mohs's Hardness Scale to identify each of your unknown minerals.

Concluding-the-Analysis Statements:

(1) I learned…

(2) If I were to re-do this lab, I would change…

(3) An example of a variable in this lab is…

(4) An example of a control in this lab is…

Part 3: (Student Handout)

Note: Distribute to students after they complete the Prediction in *Part 2*.

Anticipation Section Title: (G-2) Knowing Mohs

Thinking About the Problem

Do you know why diamonds are often used as industrial tools? The answer is that they are so hard that they can be used to cut metals and other hard objects. In fact, the gemstone diamond is the hardest known mineral. Other hard minerals include topaz and quartz. On the other hand, do you know why talcum powder is so soft? This powder comes from pulverizing the mineral talc, which is very soft. Other soft minerals include graphite and gypsum. For geologists, the hardness of a mineral is determined by how easily it can be scratched compared with other minerals on a scale called the Mohs's Hardness Scale.

Scientists use various properties—such as hardness, luster, color, and, as you already know from our Lab G-1, specific gravity (density)—to help identify minerals. In this lab, you will learn to identify a set of minerals by comparing their hardness values against known standards. Glass (with a hardness value of 5.5), copper (hardness of 3.5), and a fingernail (hardness of 2.5) are frequently used by geologists as standards.

Data Collection Materials:

- Copper (Cu) plate

- Glass (SiO_2) plate

- Hand lenses

- Iron (Fe) nail

- Six unknown mineral samples

Data Collection Procedures:

(1) Test the hardness of each mineral by using the tools at your lab station. Record your results as "yes" or "no" in Data Collection Table #1.

(2) Use Data Collection Table #2 and Data Collection Table #3 to help you estimate the Mohs's hardness value based upon your experiment results. Record your answer in each case as less than (<) or greater than (>).

(3) Check the mineral; don't wreck the mineral.

Lab Geology 3: (G-3) Classifying Rocks and Geologic Role

Part 1: (Teacher's Lesson Plan Outline)

Note: See Lesson Planning on page 32.

Anticipation Section Title: (G-3) Classifying Rocks and Geologic Role

Problem: What are the differences between igneous, sedimentary, and metamorphic rocks?

Prediction: Give a working definition of the word *rock*.

Thinking About the Problem: (See p. 106.)

Data Collection Materials and Procedures: (See p. 107.)

Note: Reviewing the Rock Cycle Diagram in Figure 3.1 is recommended at the end of Lab G-3. Student lab groups can be given the task of producing a skit that shows the rock cycle in action.

SC*i*INKS.
THE WORLD'S A CLICK AWAY
Topic: Identifying Rocks
Go to: *www.scilinks.org*
Code: ESS011

SC*i*INKS.
THE WORLD'S A CLICK AWAY
Topic: The Rock Cycle
Go to: *www.scilinks.org*
Code: ESS012

SC*i*INKS.
THE WORLD'S A CLICK AWAY
Topic: Composition of Rock
Go to: *www.scilinks.org*
Code: ESS013

Figure 3.1. The Rock Cycle Diagram

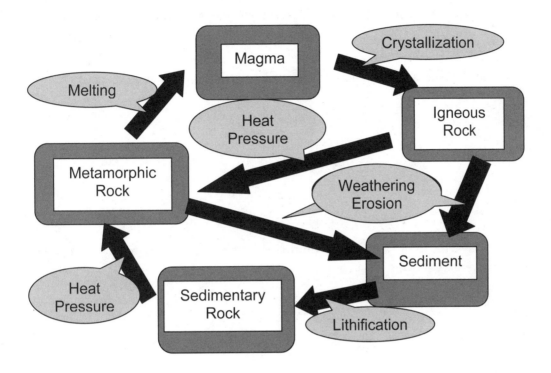

Note: **Key to rock samples:** Three igneous (obsidian–#1, basalt–#9, pumice–#5), three sedimentary (sandstone–#2, shale–#8, conglomerate–#4), and three metamorphic (quartzite–#3, slate–#7, marble–#6).

Safety Requirements: goggles

Expansion and Further Investigation:

(1) Specifically, how would you improve the Rock and Role Key (Figure 3.2), to get rid of any challenges that it presented to you?

(2) Closely examine several sedimentary rocks. In addition to sight, what other senses could help you key out the rocks?

Topic: Igneous Rock

Go to: *www.scilinks.org*

Code: ESS014

SC*LINKS*
THE WORLD'S A CLICK AWAY

Topic: Metamorphic Rock

Go to: *www.scilinks.org*

Code: ESS015

SC*LINKS*
THE WORLD'S A CLICK AWAY

Topic: Sedimentary Rock

Go to: *www.scilinks.org*

Code: ESS016

Part 2: (Student Lab Notebook Entries)

Anticipation Section Title: (G-3) Classifying Rocks and Geologic Role

Problem: What are the differences between igneous, sedimentary, and metamorphic rocks?

Prediction:

Note: Distribute the student handout (see *Part 3*) after students have completed their predictions.

Thinking About the Problem: Paraphrase the three main points of the reading in your own words.

(1)

(2)

(3)

Table 3.7. Data Collection Table #1: Classifying Rocks and Geologic Role

Rock Sample	Description of Visible Properties	Rock Classification
1		
2		
3		
4		
5		
6		
7		
8		
9		

Analysis:

(1) How are igneous and metamorphic rocks similar and different?

(2) How are sedimentary and metamorphic rocks similar and different?

(3) How are igneous and sedimentary rocks similar and different?

Concluding-the-Analysis Statements:

(1) I learned…

(2) If I were to re-do this lab, I would change…

(3) An example of a variable in this lab is…

(4) An example of a control in this lab is…

Part 3: (Student Handout)

Note: Distribute to students after they complete the Prediction in *Part 2*.

Anticipation Section Title: (G-3) Classifying Rocks and Geologic Role

---

Thinking About the Problem

What are rocks made of? A rock is a natural mixture of minerals. Of the 3,000 known minerals, only a few dozen are essential constituents of rocks. A "felsic" mineral, which is a combination of the terms *feldspar* and *silica*, is among the most common minerals that make up rocks. Examples of felsic minerals are quartz, feldspar, and mica. The other most common mineral that makes up rocks is a "mafic" mineral, which is a combination of the terms that describe magnesium and iron. Examples of mafic minerals are olivine, pyroxene, and amphibole.

There are three main groups of rocks: igneous, sedimentary, and metamorphic. These are classified by the role that the Earth played in their development. Igneous (*igneus*, "fire" in Latin) rocks develop when liquid molten rock, called magma, solidifies in the Earth's crust or on the Earth's surface. The rate at which the magma cools plays a big role in the crystal size and mineral composition.

Sedimentary (*sedere*, "to settle" in Latin) rocks develop at the Earth's surface as the weathering result of rocks exposed to wind, water, or ice. When weather and other forces of erosion wear away rocks, sediments form. Those sediments can be compacted, through the process of lithification (*lithos*, "stone" in Greek), to form sedimentary rocks.

Metamorphic (*metamorphoun*, "to change" in Greek) rocks develop through the transformation of other rocks due to great pressures or high temperatures. Those tremendously strong forces can change preexisting rocks through the process of metamorphism. Rocks remain solid during the entire process.

The rock cycle describes the roles and relationships among all three rock groups. We will study this in more detail at the end of Lab G-3. In this lab, you will use a rock classification system, called the Rock and Role Key, to determine into which group several unknown rocks fit.

Data Collection Materials:

- 9 rock samples

- Hand lens

- "Rock and Role Key"

Data Collection Procedures:

(1) Examine each rock sample carefully. Check the rock; don't wreck the rock.

(2) Complete Data Collection Table #1 with detail, using the Rock and Role Key.

(3) Determine if each rock sample is igneous, sedimentary, or metamorphic.

Figure 3.2. Rock and Role Key

Rock and Role Key

Directions: Answer each question in sequence. Observe your rock sample carefully.

(1) Is the rock made up of easily visible, separate particles (for example, crystals or sand)?

A. Particles are easily visible. [Go to step 3]

B. It is not composed of easily visible, separate particles. [Go to step 2]

(2) Is the rock completely solid, glassy, or porous (sponge-like)?

A. The rock is completely solid. [Go to step 5]

B. The rock is glassy or porous. [The rock is igneous]

(3) What types of particles make up your rock?

A. The rock is made of easily visible, shiny mineral crystals. [Go to step 4]

B. The rock is made up of sand or pebbles that appear to be cemented together. [The rock is sedimentary]

(4) Do the mineral crystals of your rock tend to line up or form different-colored bands?

A. The mineral crystals are not lined up in a particular direction. [Go to step 7]

B. The mineral crystals tend to line up or form bands. [The rock is metamorphic]

(5) Is your rock made up of visible layers, or does it tend to break into layers?

A. The rock has visible layers or tends to break into layers. [Go to step 6]

B. The rock has no layers nor does it break into layers. [The rock is igneous]

(6) How reflective or shiny is your rock?

A. The rock is quite dull, not reflective or shiny. [The rock is sedimentary]

B. The rock is fairly shiny or reflective. [The rock is metamorphic]

(7) Is your rock is made up of one or more different types or colors of mineral crystals?

A. There appear to be two or more types of mineral crystals. [The rock is igneous]

B. All of the crystals appear to be the same mineral. [The rock is metamorphic]

Lab Geology 4: (G-4) Unearthing History

Part 1: (Teacher's Lesson Plan Outline)

Note: See Lesson Planning on page 32.

Anticipation Section Title: (G-4) Unearthing History

Problem: Where do life-forms appear in a time line of Earth history?

Prediction: Answer the problem statement.

Thinking About the Problem: (See p. 113.)

Data Collection Materials and Procedures: (See p. 114.)

Expansion and Further Investigation:

(1) Observe the relationships between fossils, rock layers, and the geologic time scale. Why do you think geologists found it difficult to divide the first three eons into smaller time divisions?

(2) Research and report on the geologic history of any other planet or moon in our solar system.

SCLINKS.
THE WORLD'S A CLICK AWAY

Topic: Geologic Time Scale

Go to: *www.scilinks.org*

Code: ESS017

Part 2: (Student Lab Notebook Entries)

Anticipation Section Title: (G-4) Unearthing History

Problem: Where do life-forms appear in a time line of Earth history?

Prediction:

Note: Distribute the student handout (see *Part 3*) after students have completed their predictions.

Thinking About the Problem: Paraphrase the three main points of the reading in your own words.

(1)

(2)

(3)

Table 3.8. Data Collection Table #1: Earth History on a Rope

Geologist's Division of Earth History	How Many Millions of Years Ago It Began	Measurement on Rope (0.1 cm = 1 million years)
Chronometric Eons		
Precambrian Priscoan	4,600	460 cm
Precambrian Archean	3,800	
Precambrian Proterozoic	2,500	
Phanerozoic	544	
Eras		
Paleozoic	544	54.4 cm
Mesozoic	248	
Cenozoic	65	
Periods		
Cambrian	544	
Ordovician	490	49.0 cm
Silurian	443	
Devonian	417	
Carboniferous	354	
Permian	290	
Triassic	248	
Jurassic	206	
Cretaceous	144	
Tertiary Paleogene	65	
Tertiary Neogene	24	
Quaternary	2	
Epochs		
Paleocene	65	6.5 cm
Eocene	55	
Oligocene	34	
Miocene	24	
Pliocene	5	
Pleistocene	2	
Holocene	0.01	

Table 3.9. Data Collection Table #2: Events in Earth's History

Events	Time (Millions of Years Ago)
Continental Ice Age is over in United States	0.001
Modern humans	0.5
Early humans	2
Extinction of dinosaurs	65
Rocky Mountains begin to rise	80
Flowering plants	130
First mammal	210
Greatest mass extinction	248
First reptiles	315
First amphibians	367
First trilobite	554
First green algae	1,000
First bacteria	3,800

Analysis:

(1) Hypothesize how the geologists divided the timescale into smaller units.

(2) Where on the time line are the two major extinction events?

(3) The time from 4.6 billion years ago up until the beginning of the Phanerozoic eon is called "Precambrian Time." Find this part of your timeline. How does Precambrian Time compare in length with the rest of the geologic timescale?

(4) The Cenozoic Era is the most recent era, and it includes the present. How does the Cenozoic Era compare in length with the other eras?

Concluding-the-Analysis Statements:

(1) I learned…

(2) If I were to re-do this lab, I would change…

(3) An example of a variable in this lab is…

(4) An example of a control in this lab is…

Part 3: (Student Handout)

Note: Distribute to students after they complete the Prediction in *Part 2.*

Anticipation Section Title: (G-4) Unearthing History

Thinking About the Problem

How old is the Earth? Geologists use information from rocks, rock layers, fossils (*fossus*, "dug up" in Latin), and other natural evidence to piece together the history of our planet. Geologists consider time from the formation of the Earth to today, following a geologic timescale that breaks Earth's history into manageable pieces. Geologic time is divided and subdivided into eons, eras, periods, epochs, and ages. They have used this information to put geologic events and fossil organisms (evidence of living things) in their correct sequence on this time line. The boundaries are set by major events that have been preserved in the rock record.

More recent events can be measured in the soil, as well. For example, Earth scientists now believe that an early culture of humans, known as the Clovis people who wandered North America hunting mammoths and sloths, were wiped out by a mile-wide comet. They believe this due to evidence found in a thin layer of black soil, containing iridium from comets, which coats more than 50 sites in North America, especially near the Great Lakes.

Through research, including the use of the geologic timescale, most scientists conclude that the Earth is approximately 4.6 billion years old. You will learn more about what evidence scientists use to determine this age in Lab G-5. Compared to 4.6 billion years, living things have been around for a relatively short time. This lab will help you learn about the geologic time line for Earth and more clearly understand the various geological periods and events you will hear described in the media.

Data Collection Materials:

- Earth History on a Rope scale model measurements

- Masking tape

- Rope or twine (5 m long)

- Ruler

- Scrap paper for labels

Data Collection Procedures:

(1) Lay the rope out on the ground in front of you. At the far right end, tape the label "Present Day."

(2) Starting from the Present Day mark, measure back exactly 4.6 meters. Label this "Formation of the Earth."

(3) Measure from the Present Day mark and label each eon, era, period, and epoch (with a different color code).

(4) Use Data Collection Table #1 to label each event in Earth's history.

Lab Geology 5: (G-5) Drilling Through the Ages

Part 1: (Teacher's Lesson Plan Outline)

Note: See Lesson Planning on page 32.

Anticipation Section Title: (G-5) Drilling Through the Ages

Problem: How can we use drilling through rocks to examine geologic history?

Prediction: What methods can be used to determine the ages of rock layers?

Thinking About the Problem: (See pp. 120–121.)

Data Collection Materials and Procedures: (See p. 121.)

Expansion and Further Investigation:

(1) Find geologic maps of your local area and create a geologic profile. Present this profile to the class.

(2) Contact a local water, oil, or gas drilling company to discuss and learn from their methods of collecting data on the rock layers underground.

SCiLINKS
THE WORLD'S A CLICK AWAY

Topic: Geologic
Periods and Epochs

Go to: *www.scilinks.org*

Code: ESS018

Part 2: (Student Lab Notebook Entries)

Anticipation Section Title: (G-5) Drilling Through the Ages

Problem: How can we use drilling through rocks to examine geologic history?

Prediction:

Note: Distribute the student handout (see *Part 3*) after students have completed their predictions.

Thinking About the Problem: Paraphrase the three main points of the reading in your own words.

(1)

(2)

(3)

Table 3.10. Data Collection Table #1: Water Wells A, B, and C

Water Well A		
Depth (m)	**Rock**	**Geologist Notes**
12	Shale	
16	Conglomerate	
25	Sandstone	135 million years old (index fossils found)
30	Impermeable shale	No date available
45	Breccia	
53	Sandstone	
58	Shale	
Water Well B		
Depth (m)	**Rock**	**Geologist Notes**
15	Shale	21 million years old (Index fossils found)
16	Conglomerate	
23	Sandstone	
26	Impermeable shale	
45	Breccia	
51	Sandstone	280 million years old (radioactive dating)
60	Shale	310 million years old (index fossils found)
70	Schist	385 million years old (radioactive dating)
76	Marble	
85	Basalt	
Water Well C		
Depth (m)	**Rock**	**Geologist Notes**
5	Sandstone	0.5 million years old (radioactive dating)
18	Shale	
21	Conglomerate	51 million years old (index fossils found)
25	Sandstone	
34	Impermeable shale	
47	Breccia	230 million years old (index fossils found)
55	Sandstone	
63	Shale	
70	Schist	
75	Marble	405 million years old (radioactive dating)
81	Basalt	460 million years old (radioactive dating)

Table 3.11. Data Collection Table #2: Ages of Each Rock Layer

Number of Rock Layer	Era	Period	Age of Rock Layer	Method Used to Determine Age	Type of Rock
1	Cenozoic	Quaternary	0.5 million years	Radioactive	Sandstone
2					
3					
4					
5					
6					
7					
8					
9					
10					
11					

Table 3.12. Data Collection Table #3: Geologic Time Table

Millions of Years Ago	Era	Period
0–2	Cenozoic	Quaternary
2–24	Cenozoic	Tertiary Neogene
24–65	Cenozoic	Tertiary Paleogene
65–141	Mesozoic	Cretaceous
141–195	Mesozoic	Jurassic
195–230	Mesozoic	Triassic
230–280	Paleozoic	Permian
280–310	Paleozoic	Pennsylvanian
310–345	Paleozoic	Mississippian
345–395	Paleozoic	Devonian
395–435	Paleozoic	Silurian
435–500	Paleozoic	Ordovician
500–570	Paleozoic	Cambrian

Analysis:

(1) Explain one other way to find out the age of the rock in layer #5 (Table 3.11).

(2) Explain whether or not all of the similar rock types are found at the same depth.

(3) Describe the difference between the relative age of a rock layer and its absolute age.

Concluding-the-Analysis Statements:

(1) I learned…

(2) If I were to re-do this lab, I would change…

(3) An example of a variable in this lab is…

(4) An example of a control in this lab is…

Part 3: (Student Handout)

Note: Distribute to students after they complete the Prediction in *Part 2*.

Anticipation Section Title: (G-5) Drilling Through the Ages

Thinking About the Problem

Why are geologists interested in drilling? Geologists work together with engineers when drilling for groundwater wells. Drilling allows geologists to examine where different layers of rock begin and end. In the search for water, geologists frequently look for a layer of sandstone perched above a layer of impermeable shale.

Geologists also have an interest in drilling, because rock layers provide a record of events that have occurred on Earth. They can contain the remains and/or imprints of the different plants and animals that have lived on Earth.

As you learned in Lab G-4, scientists estimate that the Earth is approxi-mately 4.6 billion years old. There are many pieces of supporting evidence for this. One piece of supporting evidence is the thickness of the rock layers on Earth. Although, in terms of accuracy, it is not the most effective method, scientists can perform experiments to determine how long it takes to create one meter of a particular rock type. They then multiply this time by the actual thickness of those particular rock layers on Earth. This allows scientists to roughly esti-mate the age of the Earth. Most geologists believe that it would have taken ap-proximately 4.6 billion years to generate all the layers of rock found on Earth. This study of rock layer depths has been backed up by much more accurate evidence from radioactive minerals and index fossils in the rocks.

Earth scientists study the evidence associated with when the continents began to solidify. Newly discovered Greenland outcrops (an ancient piece of the sea floor, which was raised up by crustal movement) are among the oldest mea-sured, at 3.8 billion years, while most of the continents are much younger, at 2.5 billion years old.

By understanding some simple rules about rock layer formation, we can use the layers and the associated rock types to measure the amount of time that has passed. One important thing to remember is that rock layers form hori-zontally. A second important factor is that the older rocks will normally be found farther beneath the surface, while younger rocks will normally be clos-er to the top. This allows scientists to use the positions underground to deter-mine the "age based on position."   (cont.)

Thinking About the Problem (cont.)

Scientists can use index fossils to determine the "relative age" of layers. Index fossils are the remains of a single species that are so widespread and well-known (age-wise) that its fossils enable geologists to correlate environments and time. They can also measure the radioactive minerals found in a rock layer to determine the "absolute age" of the layer.

There are many deep wells (water, oil, etc.) available for geologists to examine. This lab uses the scenario of three water wells, drilled within five kilometers of each other.

Data Collection Materials:

- Drilling Through the Ages Diagram (Figure 3.3)

- Metric ruler

Data Collection Procedures:

(1) At each drilling site marked on the Drilling Through the Ages diagram, place a small horizontal line at the depths described in Data Collection Table #1. Write the name of the rock on that line. The first line for Water Well C, sandstone, has been done for you.

(2) Draw a line across the page to connect the areas on all three wells where the rock layers are the same.

(3) Use the notes from Data Collection Table #1 to determine the age of each rock layer. Write the age underneath each line.

(4) Complete Data Collection Table #2 in order from youngest (1) to oldest (11).

Figure 3.3. Drilling Through the Ages Diagram

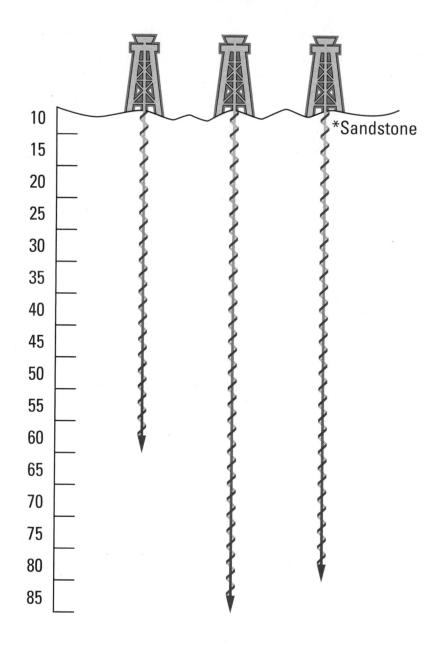

*Sandstone

Lab Geology 6: (G-6) Hunting Through the Sand

Part 1: (Teacher's Lesson Plan Outline)

Note: See Lesson Planning on page 32.

Anticipation Section Title: (G-6) Hunting Through the Sand

Problem: Can you identify the rocks and minerals in sand?

Prediction: Describe the materials that can be found in sand.

Thinking About the Problem: (See p. 126.)

Data Collection Materials and Procedures: (See p. 126.)

Expansion and Further Investigation:

(1) Research anything you can learn about the soil profile in the community near your home (prior to development may be easier to find). Use the library to find your "County/Province Soil Survey." Use the Soil and Water Conservation District or the University Extension Service. Report your findings to the class.

(2) Take a sample of your soil to a gardening store for analysis. Learn what the acidity level is, as well as what the percentages of nitrogen, potassium, and phosphorus are.

SCiLINKS
THE WORLD'S A CLICK AWAY
Topic: Soil Types
Go to: *www.scilinks.org*
Code: ESS019

Part 2: (Student Lab Notebook Entries)

Anticipation Section Title: (G-6) Hunting Through the Sand

Problem: Can you identify the rocks and minerals in sand?

Prediction:

Note: Distribute the student handout (see *Part 3*) after students have completed their predictions.

Thinking About the Problem: Paraphrase the three main points of the reading in your own words.

(1)

(2)

(3)

Table 3.13. Data Collection Table #1: Hunting Through the Sand

Organic materials (Remains of dead plants)	Magnetite (Black or brown, rounded pebbles, magnetic)	Limestone (White to light brown, not shiny)
Granite (Different colors, made up of several types of crystals, larger)	My sandbox	Mica (Clear to smoky dark, shiny, thin sheets or flakes)
Quartz (Different colors, shiny, looks like glass)	Slate (Black to gray, not shiny, tiny angular crystals)	Feldspar (White to light brown, jagged or sharp, not shiny)

Analysis:

(1) Describe the various materials that make up sand.

(2) Describe any challenges that you had in sorting your sand grains.

Concluding-the-Analysis Statements:

(1) I learned…

(2) If I were to re-do this lab, I would change…

(3) An example of a variable in this lab is…

(4) An example of a control in this lab is…

Part 3: (Student Handout)

Note: Distribute to students after they complete the Prediction in *Part 2.*

Anticipation Section Title: (G-6) Hunting Through the Sand

Thinking About the Problem

Why do flowers grow well in one soil but not in another? Soils are typically composed of 45% minerals, 25% air, 25% water, and 5% organic matter. In general, the more organic matter, the better the flowers grow, but proper amounts of air, water, and trace minerals are important too.

Soil textures (*textus*, "woven" in Latin) are determined by the percentages of clay, silt, and sand that are found in the soil. In Lab G-5 we studied rock layers. Like rocks, soils are also found in layers. A description of this layering is called a "soil profile."

As you go deeper in the soil, you find lesser amounts of partly decayed organic matter and greater amounts of partially weathered bedrock material. All rocks that are exposed at Earth's surface are subject to weathering, which leads to the formation of sediments. Forces of erosion (primarily water and wind) can transport sediments around Earth's surface. Erosion and weathering form soil. In this lab you will examine the various materials that make up the sand that is found in a soil sample.

Data Collection Materials:

- Glue

- Hand lens

- Hunting Through the Sand data table

- Pinch of sand

- Toothpick

Data Collection Procedures:

(1) Place a pinch of sand in the center of your Hunting Through the Sand data table.

(2) Put a small drop of glue on a paper towel, using the toothpick to apply it when needed.

(3) Use the hand lens to sort the sand grains according to the descriptions on your Hunting Through the Sand data table. Glue each grain down to the proper spot.

Lab Geology 7: (G-7) Shaking Things Up

Part 1: (Teacher's Lesson Plan Outline)

Note: See Lesson Planning on page 32.

Anticipation Section Title: (G-7) Shaking Things Up

Problem: Why do earthquakes happen in certain locations around the world?

Prediction: Describe, in one sentence, where you think most earthquakes in the world will occur over the next two months.

Note: It may be helpful, prior to beginning the data collection portion of Lab G-7, to review the structure of the Earth. When drilling into the Earth (as you saw in Lab G-5), scientists do not go very deep relative to all of the layers of the Earth. The scientists dig down into the crust only. The surface layers of the Earth are where sand is found (as in Lab G-6). Earthquakes, which we refer to in this lab, can go very deep into the crustal plates, but they still do not go below the thickness of the line shown in Figure 3.4 below. The structure of the Earth diagram (see Figure 3.4) was determined primarily through validations of evidence included in the theory of plate tectonics.

Figure 3.4. Structure of the Earth

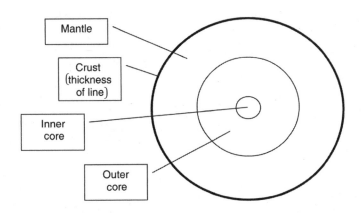

Note: According to the U.S. Geological Survey Earthquake Hazards Program, "The magnitude of an earthquake is determined from the logarithm of the amplitude of waves recorded by seismographs. On the Richter Scale, magnitude is expressed in whole numbers and decimal fractions. For example, a magnitude 5.3 might be computed for a moderate earthquake, and a strong earthquake might be rated as magnitude 6.3. Because of the logarithmic basis of the scale, each whole number increase in magnitude represents a tenfold increase in measured amplitude; as an estimate of energy, each whole number step in the magnitude scale corresponds to the release of about 31 times more energy than the amount associated with the preceding whole number value." (Visit *http://earthquake.usgs.gov* for more information.)

Thinking About the Problem: (See p. 131.)

Data Collection Materials and Procedures: (See p. 132.)

Expansion and Further Investigation:

(1) Follow a similar procedure to trace subduction zones by noticing depths of earthquakes (in 100 km increments). Show the class your world map, explaining the patterns that you find. Explain the cause and effect relationship between plate tectonics and earthquakes.

(2) Research and report on a fault zone in the United States, sharing especially any future predictions for activity levels.

(3) Develop a presentation on building materials and methods that are designed to sustain earthquakes without damage.

Topic: Earth's Structure
Go to: *www.scilinks.org*
Code: ESS020

Topic: Earthquakes
Go to: *www.scilinks.org*
Code: ESS021

Topic: Earthquake Measurement
Go to: *www.scilinks.org*
Code: ESS022

Part 2: (Student Lab Notebook Entries)

Anticipation Section Title: (G-7) Shaking Things Up

Problem: Why do earthquakes happen in certain locations around the world?

Prediction:

Note: Distribute the student handout (see *Part 3*) after students have completed their prediction.

Thinking About the Problem: Paraphrase the three main points of the reading in your own words.

(1)

(2)

(3)

Figure 3.5. Data Collection Table #1: Map of the World

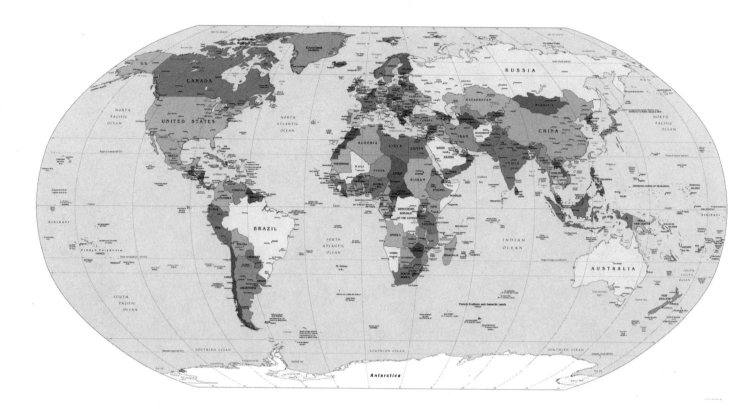

Analysis:

(1) Describe how your map of the world has changed over the course of two months.

(2) What patterns do you notice in terms of the locations of earthquakes?

(3) What patterns do you notice in terms of the magnitudes of earthquakes?

Concluding-the-Analysis Statements:

(1) I learned…

(2) If I were to re-do this lab, I would change…

(3) An example of a variable in this lab is…

(4) An example of a control in this lab is…

Part 3: (Student Handout)

Note: Distribute to students after they complete the Prediction in *Part 2.*

Anticipation Section Title: (G-7) Shaking Things Up

Thinking About the Problem

Can you predict earthquakes? Scientists have never predicted a major earthquake. They do not know how, and they do not expect to know how any time soon. However, probabilities, based on scientific data, can be calculated for potential future earthquakes. Scientists are becoming better and better at predicting the likelihood of potential earthquakes.

Plates are the slabs of the Earth's crust that make up the lithosphere (*lithos,* "stone" in Greek). Geologists developed the plate tectonic theory as a model of movement of Earth's crust on the surface. Earth's crust is composed of the continental crust (30 to 100 km thick) and the oceanic crust (about 10 km thick). Faults (*fallere,* "to fail" in Latin) are fractures in the Earth's crust caused by the stresses of plate movements.

The word *earthquake* is used to describe any seismic (*seismos,* "earthquake" in Greek) event—whether a natural phenomenon or something caused by humans—that generates seismic waves. Seismic waves are caused mostly by the rupture of geological faults, but also by volcanic activity, landslides, mine blasts, and nuclear experiments. An earthquake is usually the result of a sudden release of energy in Earth's crust, due to slippage along geologic faults, causing a vibration of the Earth.

There are many misconceptions about earthquakes. Some believe that animals predict earthquakes. Unresearched evidence does exist of animals, such as fish, birds, reptiles, and insects, exhibiting strange behavior anywhere from weeks to seconds before an earthquake occurs. However, consistent and reliable behavior prior to seismic events has never been shown.

Earthquakes may occur near a volcanic eruption, but they are the result of the active forces connected with the eruption, and not the cause of volcanic activity. Also, contrary to some beliefs, earthquakes are equally as likely to occur at any time of the day or month or year.

Geologists use the Richter scale to assign magnitude to earthquakes by the height of the largest seismic wave that each earthquake creates. Each unit of additional magnitude refers to a tenfold increase in the level of ground shaking and an even more dramatic increase in energy. For example, a magnitude 7.0 earthquake has more than 30 times more energy than a magnitude 6.0.

Data Collection Materials:

- Colored pencils

- Internet access to the U.S. Geological Survey's earthquake page

- Pushpins of different colors

- Wall-size map of the world

Data Collection Procedures:

(1) Post a map of the world on a bulletin board in the classroom.

(2) Each student should glue a smaller world map in his or her lab notebook (Figure 3.5).

(3) Visit the U.S. Geological Survey's "Current Worldwide Earthquake List" on the internet (*http://earthquake.usgs.gov/regional/neic*).

(4) Put a pushpin in the wall map where any earthquakes have occurred that day. Repeat this pattern daily (assign students this job at the beginning of class time).

(5) Students use colored pencils to indicate the same information in their lab notebooks.

(6) Use different colors to indicate magnitudes of earthquakes (strong, medium, and weak).

Lab Geology 8: (G-8) Mounting Magma

Part 1: (Teacher's Lesson Plan Outline)

Note: See Lesson Planning on page 32.

Anticipation Section Title: (G-8) Mounting Magma

Problem: How do different types of volcanoes differ from one another?

Prediction: Describe, in one sentence, the differences between cinder cone, shield volcanoes, and stratovolcanoes.

Thinking About the Problem: (See p. 138.)

Data Collection Materials and Procedures: (See p. 139.)

Note: The model volcano that students build is a stratovolcano.

Safety Requirements: goggles, aprons

Expansion and Further Investigation:

(1) Research Mount St. Helens, Mount Ranier, Mount Shasta, Mount Mazama, and Redoubt Volcano, all of which are stratovolcanoes. Report your findings to the class in poster form with descriptive headings on the qualifications of each volcano.

(2) What are some problems and hazards that townspeople who live at the foot of volcanic mountains face? Design a plan for possible solutions to these problems.

(3) Investigate what types of rocks are produced by each of the types of volcanoes (cinder cone, shield volcanoes, and stratovolcanoes) mentioned in this lab.

(4) Using the map that you developed for Lab G-7, plot all of the recently active volcanoes on Earth. What patterns do you notice? Explain where the magma comes from for volcanoes.

(5) Using the concepts you learned during our unit on astronomy, what planets or moons in our solar system show evidence of volcanic activity? What types of data are collected as evidence?

SC*LINKS.*
THE WORLD'S A CLICK AWAY

Topic: Volcanoes

Go to: *www.scilinks.org*

Code: ESS023

SC*LINKS.*
THE WORLD'S A CLICK AWAY

Topic: Types of Volcanoes

Go to: *www.scilinks.org*

Code: ESS024

Part 2: (Student Lab Notebook Entries)

Anticipation Section Title: (G-8) Mounting Magma

Problem: How do different types of volcanoes differ from one another?

Prediction:

Note: Distribute the student handout (see *Part 3*) after students have completed their predictions.

Thinking About the Problem: Paraphrase the three main points of the reading in your own words.

(1)

(2)

(3)

Figure 3.6. Data Collection Table #1: Volcano Pattern

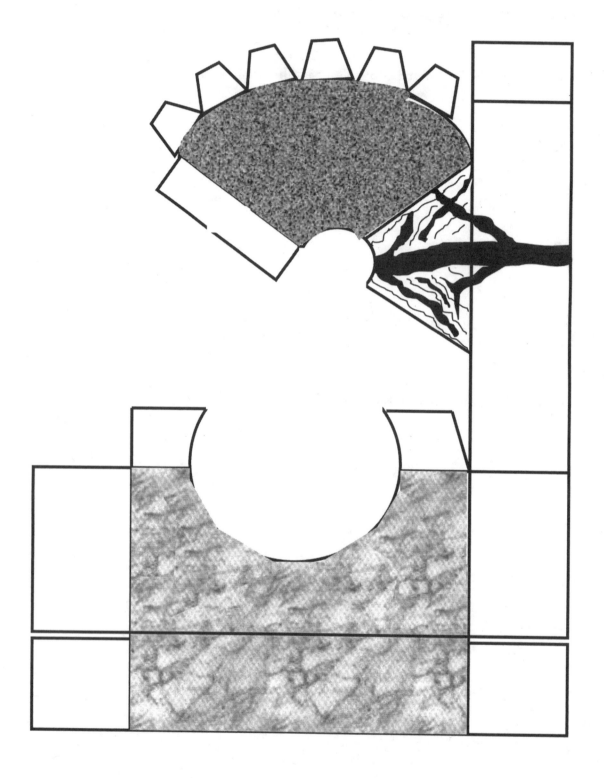

Analysis:

(1) Which liquid—warm water or cold water—produced the best simulation of a volcanic eruption? Why?

(2) Make three detailed observations about your results from this experiment.

(3) After studying the results, which type of volcano has been produced?

(4) Compare and contrast your results with those of the other lab groups. Describe what you notice.

Concluding-the-Analysis Statements:

(1) I learned…

(2) If I were to re-do this lab, I would change…

(3) An example of a variable in this lab is…

(4) An example of a control in this lab is…

Part 3: (Student Handout)

Note: Distribute to students after they complete the Prediction in *Part 2*.

Anticipation Section Title: (G-8) Mounting Magma

Thinking About the Problem

Are all volcanoes alike? Volcanoes form where magma burns through the crust, at subduction (*sub* + *ducere*, "to lead under" in Latin) zones, at spreading centers, or at "hot spots" like Hawaii. Volcanoes have two major sections. The crater is the pit at the top portion of the volcano. The vent is a pipelike structure that connects the underground magma chamber to the crater.

Scientists classify the three types of volcanoes as shield volcanoes, cinder cones, and stratovolcanoes (also known as composite volcanoes). Shield volcanoes are the largest of all volcano types. They are generally not explosive and are built by the accumulation of lava flows that spread out widely. Lava flows that spread are very fluid and are described as having low viscosity. Viscosity refers to the level of ease with which a fluid flows. Shield volcanoes form broad, gentle slopes, and can be tens of kilometers across and thousands of meters high. Kilauea and Mauna Loa Volcanoes in Hawaii are examples of active shield volcanoes.

Cinder cones are the smallest. They have steep sides that are formed mainly by the piling up of ash, cinders, and rocks. All of these materials explosively erupted from the vent of the volcano and are called pyroclastic, which means "fire-broken." The cinders shoot out of the volcano like fireworks, and then fall back to the ground. As they fall, they pile up to form a symmetrical, steep-sided cone around the vent. Sunset Crater in Arizona and Paricutin in Mexico are well-known examples of cinder cones.

A stratovolcano is the most common type of volcano on Earth. Also called a composite volcano, it is built up of lava flows layered with pyroclastic material. Scientists believe that the layering represents a history of alternating explosive and quiet eruptions. Young stratovolcanoes are typically steep-sided and symmetrically cone-shaped. There are many active stratovolcanoes in North America, including Mount St. Helens in Washington. Other well-known stratovolcanoes include Mount Ranier, Mount Shasta, Mount Mazama (Crater Lake), Redoubt Volcano in Alaska, Mount Fuji in Japan, and Mount Vesuvius in Italy.

In this lab, you will put together a model of a volcano. You will use it to test what type of volcano results from your simulated chemical volcanic eruption.

Data Collection Materials:

- Film canister (one per lab group)

- Scissors

- Two Alka-Seltzer tablets

- Volcano pattern (one per student)

- Water (both warm and cold)

Data Collection Procedures:

(1) Cut out the volcano pattern, along the outer lines.

(2) Fold the model volcano along the inner lines, and then tape the tabs together.

(3) Place the empty film canister in the center of the cone.

(4) Cut your Alka-Seltzer tablets in half, enabling you to conduct repeated trials. Place one Alka-Seltzer piece and one drop of red food coloring into the film canister.

(5) Quickly add some cold water to the canister and watch the mounting magma.

(6) Use your lab partner's volcano model, and repeat step 4. Then quickly add some warm water to the canister and watch.

(7) Study the results and, along with determining the effect of water temperature on reaction rates, also determine which type of volcano your model represents.

Chapter 4

Meteorology

*N*ote to the teacher: Students investigate Earth's atmosphere, beginning with a study of the hydrologic cycle. They examine how factors such as pressure, saturation, and air density contribute to weather. Students are introduced to concepts of air masses and the ways these masses interact to produce weather. Students examine patterns, using them to make predictions and forecasts about weather conditions.

The 10-day outline (Table 4.1), assumes that your course started with the Pretest for Earth Science, Lab S-1, and the astronomy unit. If, however, you choose to cover Meteorology first, we recommend that you still begin with the Pretest and Lab S-1 (see Chapter 1, "The First Ten Days").

Table 4.1. Possible Syllabus for the First Ten Days of Meteorology.

Week 1	Day 1	Day 2	Day 3	Day 4	Day 5
	KWL flip book, Lab M-1 (anticipation)	Lab M-1 (data collection)	"Oh, the Science-Related Places…" assigned (Appendix B), Lab M-1 (analysis)	"Wondering About Water" classroom work time	Lab M-2 (anticipation)
Week 2	**Day 1**	**Day 2**	**Day 3**	**Day 4**	**Day 5**
	Lab M-1 (report due), Lab M-2 (Weather Watch Data Sheet preparation)	Lab M-2 (weather report data collection), Lab M-3 (anticipation)	Lab M-2 (weather report data collection), Lab M-3 (data collection)	Lab M-2 (weather report data collection), Lab M-3 (analysis) Pop Can Implosion demo	Lab M-2 (weather report data collection), Lab M-3 (report due)

Lab Meteorology 1: (M-1) Wondering About Water

Part 1: (Teacher's Lesson Plan Outline)

Note: See Lesson Planning on page 32.

Anticipation Section Title: (M-1) Wondering About Water

Problem: How does the hydrologic cycle affect the world around me (see Figure 4.1)?

Prediction: Describe, in one sentence, the answer to the problem statement.

Thinking About the Problem: (See p. 148.)

Data Collection Materials and Procedures: (See p. 149.)

Figure 4.1. Hydrologic Cycle

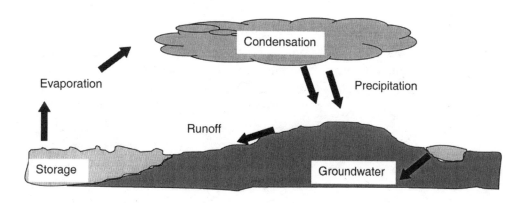

- *Note:* The comic book template, in Data Collection Table #2, is for idea generation only. Teachers can decide whether they want to simply present this via transparency or require students to match the template completely with their comic book.

- *Note:* See Water Wonders, (Figure 4.2). This should be provided for students as part of the summary section. You may want to make a transparency of the Water Wonders story, and read it out loud while the students follow along. The following are some, but not all, of the options for you to choose from: evaporation—condensation—precipitation; precipitation—runoff—consumed by animal; snow—melting to liquid—evaporation; river—ocean—evaporation; and precipitation—groundwater—transpiration.

- *Note:* Set up Data Collection Table #1: Hydrologic Cycle Model as shown below.

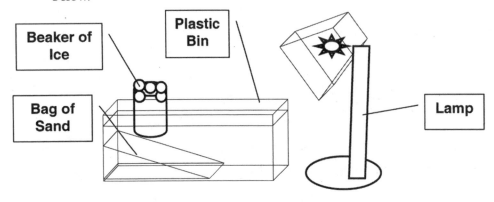

Safety Requirements: goggles, aprons

Expansion and Further Investigation:

(1) Investigate what types of devices are used to produce drinking water from ocean water. Write a detailed, half-page report on your findings.

(2) Research the percentage of time that a typical water molecule would spend in each particular phase of the water cycle. For example, if given 100 days, how many days would the water molecule spend in the ocean, in the atmosphere, in a lake, or in a cloud?

SCI
LINKS.
THE WORLD'S A CLICK AWAY

Topic: The Water Cycle
Go to: *www.scilinks.org*
Code: ESS025

Figure 4.2. Water Wonders

Water Wonders

Once upon a time, a royal family lived in a palace in the clouds. Two sisters, both water molecule princesses, were always looking for adventures. Their names were Maureen and Mary Molecule, and they were both kind-hearted, wonderful water molecules. For fun, one day, they fell to Earth as part of a raindrop with many other molecules from their kingdom.

Maureen and Mary landed in a bur oak tree, rolled over an acorn, then dripped gently to the ground. Both had many good friends with them—molecules are so very small that it took lots and lots of molecules to make up the tiny raindrop that Maureen and Mary were in.

A short time after they landed on the ground, the Sun came out. The Sun warmed the ground and all of the water molecules on it. Maureen and Mary started to feel wonderfully warm. They evaporated back into the atmosphere and eventually continued their adventures around Earth as part of the water molecule cycle.

During Maureen and Mary Molecule's many travels in the water cycle, they spent time stored on the surface of the Earth in glaciers, melting and flowing into lakes, relaxing underground among rocks and soil, and even traveling through living things. They were able to join other water molecules to become a water droplet in a cumulus cloud, freezing and falling to Earth as a snowflake. Eventually Maureen and Mary could flow to the oceans, be transpired by plants, or be evaporated directly back up into their palace in the sky.

Throughout all of Maureen and Mary Molecule's journeys, the amount of water on Earth and in our atmosphere remained the same—it just changed from solid to liquid to gas and did some traveling. You see, water molecules are pretty tough, and it is very hard to hurt them. Maureen and Mary were strong. As water molecules, they were made up of three atoms: two small hydrogen atoms (H_2), and one larger oxygen atom (O), tightly connected. Water molecules (H_2O) like Maureen and Mary, don't change their appearance when they are cooled, warmed, or under pressure. In ice, water, and water vapor, water molecules stay the same.

For the Analysis section on Lab M-1, use your creativity to describe the journey of any water molecule through any three steps of the water cycle. Make your description into a five-scene comic strip.

Part 2: (Student Lab Notebook Entries)

Anticipation Section Title: (M-1) Wondering About Water

Problem: How does the hydrologic cycle affect the world around me?

Prediction:

Note: Distribute the student handout (see *Part 3*) after students have completed their predictions.

Thinking About the Problem: Paraphrase the three main points of the reading in your own words.

 (1)

 (2)

 (3)

Table 4.2. Data Collection Table #1: Hydrologic Cycle Model

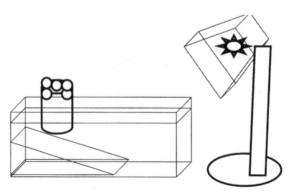

Table 4.3. Data Collection Table #2: Water Wonders Comic Book

Creative Title for Your Water Wonders Comic Book Here	
Scene one: Introduce your main character(s).	Scene two: Take your character(s) through any first step of the hydrologic cycle.
Scene three: Take your character(s) through any next step of the hydrologic cycle.	Scene four: Take your character(s) through any third step of the hydrologic cycle.
Scene five: Wrap up your comic book story, showing a final outcome for your comic book character(s).	

Analysis:

Read Water Wonders, which your teacher will provide. Use this story to help give you new ideas for describing the journey of your very own water molecule through any three steps of the hydrologic cycle. Share the water molecule's journey in a five-scene comic book.

Concluding-the-Analysis Statements:

(1) I learned…

(2) If I were to re-do this lab, I would change…

(3) An example of a variable in this lab is…

(4) An example of a control in this lab is…

Part 3: (Student Handout)

Note: Distribute to students after they complete the Prediction in *Part 2*.

Anticipation Section Title: (M-1) Wondering About Water

Thinking About the Problem

Where does the water in rain come from and where does it go? Our seemingly inexhaustible supply of water is actually used over and over again. Water moves from the ocean to air and land, and from the land to ocean and air. This continuous movement of water in a cyclic pattern is called the hydrologic (*hudro*, "water" in Greek) cycle. And it is very important in the science of meteorology (*meteoron*, "astronomical phenomenon" in Greek).

In nature, the Sun warms the water in the oceans, causing surface water to evaporate. As the water vapor rises in the atmosphere (*atmos*, "vapor" in Greek), it cools and condenses into liquid droplets. Most of these droplets continue cooling to ice crystals and snowflakes. Evaporation continues as the droplets and crystals grow in size, until they eventually fall back to Earth. Precipitation falling on Earth's surface is dependent on the temperature changes below the clouds. The precipitation collects on the land surface and may flow back to the oceans, completing the cycle.

Most of the Earth's total amount of water is contained in the oceans, a volume estimated at 1,350,000,000 km³. Other reservoirs, for example, glaciers (27,500,000 km³), groundwater (8,200,000 km³), and lakes and streams (206,700 km³), hold significant water as well. Although it is in a continuous state of change due to evaporation and precipitation, our atmosphere is estimated to hold 13,000 km³ of water.

In this lab, you will study a model of how the hydrologic cycle occurs. As far as water is concerned, Earth is basically a closed system that, in this case, is represented by a clear plastic bin. A soil bag serves as a continent, a lamp as the Sun, and water as the oceans. A beaker of ice represents the cold regions of the upper atmosphere, where water vapor condenses into water droplets.

Data Collection Materials:

- Clear plastic bin

- Glass pitcher

- Ice cubes

- Lamp

- Resealable plastic bag with sand

- Water

Data Collection Procedures:

(1) Label each of the materials in the demonstration diagram shown in Data Collection Table #1, showing not only what they materials truly are, but also what each material represents in terms of the hydrologic cycle.

(2) Carefully observe the progression of events. Draw and label a sketch showing the movement of water through the hydrologic cycle by showing what the demonstration model actually represents.

Lab Meteorology 2: (M-2) Dealing With Pressure

Part 1: (Teacher's Lesson Plan Outline)

Note: See Lesson Planning on page 32.

Anticipation Section Title: (M-2) Dealing With Pressure

Problem: How does the weight of the air affect you?

Prediction: Describe, in one sentence, your best answer to this problem statement.

Thinking About the Problem: (See p. 154.)

Data Collection Materials and Procedures: (See p. 155.)

Safety Requirements: goggles, aprons

Description of Pop Can Implosion Data Collection Procedures:

(1) Pour a splash of water into the bottom of an empty pop (soda) can.

(2) Using the beaker tongs, hold the pop can on a hot plate (high temp) until you hear the water boiling and you see the steam escaping.

(3) Very quickly, invert the pop can into the shallow pan of water.

(4) The rapid motion of the steam circulates and pushes a lot of molecules out of the can, so that when it is inverted (and therefore sealed off), the pressure on the outside of the can is greater than on the inside. This causes the can to implode.

Expansion and Further Investigation:

(1) Based on your observations of the pop can in step 7, in which direction(s) is air pressure being exerted? Draw and label a picture representing your explanation and explain the phenomenon of air pressure in your own words.

(2) Explain why we usually do not feel the pressure of the atmosphere around us. When do we feel air pressure? Use resources to find the exact amount of atmospheric pressure being exerted on you at sea level.

*SCi*LINKS.
THE WORLD'S A CLICK AWAY

Topic: Atmospheric Pressure

Go to: *www.scilinks.org*

Code: ESS026

Part 2: (Student Lab Notebook Entries)

Anticipation Section Title: (M-2) Dealing With Pressure

Problem: How does the weight of the air affect you?

Prediction:

Note: Distribute the student handout (see *Part 3*) after students have completed their predictions.

Thinking About the Problem: Paraphrase the three main points of the reading in your own words.

(1)

(2)

(3)

Table 4.4. Data Collection Table #1: Air Pressure Data

Procedure 1	
Procedure 2	
Procedure 3	
Procedure 4	
Procedure 5	
Procedure 6	

Analysis:

(1) In procedure 2, what caused the events you observed to happen?

(2) In procedures 3–5, what happened to the index card? Explain with detail and give a reason why.

(3) Explain why the events occurred as they did in procedure 6.

(4) Explain, in your own words, why the pop can implodes.

Concluding-the-Analysis Statements:

(1) I learned…

(2) If I were to re-do this lab, I would change…

(3) An example of a variable in this lab is…

(4) An example of a control in this lab is…

Part 3: (Student Handout)

Note: Distribute to students after they complete the Prediction in *Part 2.*

Anticipation Section Title: (M-2) Dealing With Pressure

Thinking About the Problem

How much does air weigh? If the question seems funny at first, it's because we have lived our whole lives exposed to the weight of the atmosphere and therefore we are usually oblivious to its effect on us. Air does have weight, yet we don't often notice it. We are much more aware of the weight of water when we dive underwater, and deep-sea divers need to protect themselves in order to avoid the life-threatening respiratory and circulatory system condition called the bends. Divers suffer from the bends because the high pressure of the water causes the nitrogen to dissolve in their blood. If the diver rises too quickly, the nitrogen bursts out of solution.

The weight of the air on Earth's surface produces air pressure. Pressure (*pressus,* "pressed" in Latin) is a measure of the force over a certain area that the air is exerting due to its weight. Without it, we would certainly notice the results. Basically, we, as well as every other closed system on Earth, would soon explode without any atmospheric pressure. The instrument used to measure atmospheric pressure is called a barometer and it is essential in weather forecasting. This lab will give you an opportunity to see that air pressure, caused by the weight of the atmosphere, can produce some amazing results.

Data Collection Materials:

- Beaker tongs

- Bucket

- Empty pop cans

- Hot plate

- Index card

- Pushpin

- Shallow pan of water

- Test tube

- Water

Data Collection Procedures:

(1) Fill your test tube to the rim with water. Make a prediction about what will happen when you turn the test tube upside down.

(2) Turn the test tube over. What did you observe?

(3) Fill it with water again. Cover it with the index card, and make a tight seal. Predict what will happen when you turn the test tube upside down.

(4) Use your finger to hold the index card on, and then flip the test tube upside down. Slowly remove your hand from the index card. What did you observe?

(5) Slowly, lean the test tube on its side and record your observations.

(6) Slowly turn the test tube so that it is upside-down again. Poke a hole in it with the pin, and record your observations.

(7) Observe the imploding pop can demo by your teacher.

Lab Meteorology 3: (M-3) Phasing In Changes

Part 1: (Teacher's Lesson Plan Outline)

Note: See Lesson Planning on page 32.

Anticipation Section Title: (M-3) Phasing In Changes

Gas Bubble Introductory Activity

Note: This introductory activity is used to introduce layering in the atmosphere by describing densities of various gases. Supplementary resources (such as textbooks, media center, and internet) can be used to show atmospheric layers (e.g., stratosphere), so that students can include a diagram in their lab notebooks (see Figure 4.3). The tie-in to the follow-up lab for M-3 is the changes in density that water undergoes as its temperature changes. Each phase for water has a different density.

Problem: Which of five gases (air, carbon dioxide, helium, methane, and propane) is the densest?

Prediction: Give your best answer to the problem statement.

Figure 4.3. Atmospheric Layer Sample Diagram (not to scale)

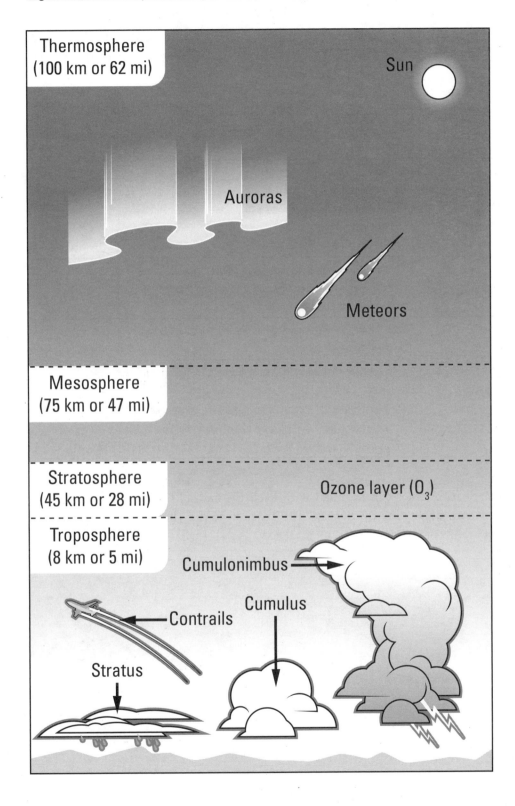

Table 4.5. Teacher Notes for Data Collection Table #1

Gas	Characteristics	Density Ranking
Carbon dioxide CO_2	Bubbles bounce. -110 °F Cloudy, due to condensation. No smell. Sinks. Strong. Puts out fires. Frozen "sublimes" to gas. Burning one gallon of gasoline emits 19.6 pounds of CO_2.	1 (most dense)
Air 78% N_2 21% O_2 0.5% H_2O 0.03% CO_2	Bubbles break when they hit things. Float and then sink. Medium strength. Clear. For humans to live, we need 12% to 58% oxygen in our air.	3
Propane C_3H_8	Flammable. Clear. Has an odor chemical added to enable detection of leaks. Sinks. Bounces, then breaks. Strong. Sometimes called "liquid petroleum."	1 (most dense)
Helium He	Floats. Breaks easily. No smell. Clear. Second most abundant gas in universe, after hydrogen.	5 (least dense)

Methane
CH_4
	Has an odor chemical added to enable detection of leaks. Floats.
	Flammable.
	Clear. Medium strength. Breaks when hits things. Sometimes
	    called "natural gas." One kilogram of CH_4 warms the Earth 23
	    times as much as one kg of CO_2.
		4

Note: Soap bubbles can be filled with each gas and allowed to drift upward or downward, depending on density. The teacher guides the students through the observations of characteristics.

Phase Changes in Water Follow-Up Lab:

Problem: What are the two things that can happen when heat is added to water?

Prediction: Answer the problem question above.

Note: Remember to have students write their predictions prior to giving them the handout.

Thinking About the Problem: (See p. 163.)

Data Collection Materials and Procedures: (See p. 164.)

Safety Requirements: goggles, aprons, and fire extinguisher nearby

Expansion and Further Investigation:

(1) Investigate what the addition of salt does to the temperature versus time graph of phase changes in water. Does saltwater have a different result?

(2) What if ice did not float on liquid water? Water is quite unique in that its solid form is less dense than its liquid form. Some scientists have hypothesized that life, as we know it, could not exist if this unique pattern were not true. Imagine and explain the ramifications for our planet.

SC*LINKS*.
THE WORLD'S A CLICK AWAY
Topic: Layers of the Atmosphere
Go to: *www.scilinks.org*
Code: ESS027

SC*LINKS*.
THE WORLD'S A CLICK AWAY
Topic: Phase Change
Go to: *www.scilinks.org*
Code: ESS028

Part 2: (Student Lab Notebook Entries)

Anticipation Section Title: (M-3) Phasing In Changes

Gas Bubble Introductory Activity

Problem: Which of five gases (air, carbon dioxide, helium, methane, and propane) is the densest?

Prediction:

Table 4.6. Data Collection Table #1: (Student should provide a title)

Gas	Characteristics	Density Ranking
Carbon dioxide		
Air		
Propane		
Helium		
Methane		

Phase Changes in Water Follow-Up Lab:

Problem: What are the two things that can happen when heat is added to water?

Prediction:

Note: Distribute the student handout (see *Part 3*) after students have completed their predictions.

Thinking About the Problem: Paraphrase the three main points of the reading in your own words.

(1)

(2)

(3)

Table 4.7. Sketch for Procedure #2

Table 4.8. Sketch for Procedure #3

Analysis:

(1) Does the addition of heat always raise the temperature of water? Give examples.

(2) Describe exactly what is happening when the water changes phase.

(a) From liquid to gas:

(b) From solid to liquid:

(3) Give a working definition of heat.

(4) Give a working definition of temperature.

Concluding-the-Analysis Statements:

(1) I learned…

(2) If I were to re-do this lab, I would change…

(3) An example of a variable in this lab is…

(4) An example of a control in this lab is…

Part 3: (Student Handout)

Note: Distribute to students after they complete the Prediction in *Part 2*.

Anticipation Section Title: (M-3) Phasing In Changes

Thinking About the Problem

What happens when you heat water? There are two main things that happen when heat is added to water. The first is that the temperature of the water rises, or increases. The second is that a "change of phase" may occur. A phase change refers to whether a substance, like water, is a solid (ice), liquid (water), or a gas (water vapor).

Several familiar terms are associated with changes of phase. *Freezing* refers to a change from liquid to solid. *Melting* refers to a change from solid to liquid. *Boiling* refers to a change from liquid to gas. *Condensing* refers to a change from gas to liquid. In the introductory activity, you saw that sometimes a substance, like carbon dioxide (its solid form is called *dry ice* because it does not melt into a liquid) may skip a step. *Sublimation* refers to these cases, when a substance goes directly from solid to gas.

In each phase change, it is the spacing between the molecules that make up the substance that changes. In a solid, the molecules (*molecula*, "small bit" in Latin) are packed very closely together. The molecules are still moving, in a shivering fashion, vibrating back and forth. In a liquid (such as water or steam), the space between molecules increases to the point where they can flow around one another. In a gas, like the invisible water vapor in our air, the molecules dart around freely, occasionally colliding with each other.

A graph of your data from this lab will show that temperatures stop increasing when phase changes are occurring. There is a leveling out of the temperature because all of the heat energy is going into the motion of the molecules. Once the molecules have separated to the distance needed for the substance to become a different phase, the temperature begins to measure this new molecular motion.

Data Collection Materials:

- Air
- Apron
- Beakers
- Bunsen burner
- Bunsen burner
- Dry ice (solid carbon dioxide)
- Gloves
- Goggles

- Helium
- Ice (or snow, as a substitute)
- Metal thermometer
- Methane
- Propane
- Small aquarium
- Soap-blown bubbles
- Water

Data Collection Procedures:

(1) Create two of your own data collection tables, giving them titles. One should show temperature versus time for water boiling. The other should show temperature versus time for ice/snow melting. Time should be recorded in 30-second intervals.

(2) Begin to measure water going from room temperature to a rolling boil. Record data on temperature every 30 seconds. The water should be allowed to boil for three minutes.

(3) At the same time, measure water with ice cubes, or snow, going to water with all the ice/snow melted. The water should continue to be measured for temperature until all the ice has been melted for three minutes.

(4) Make a line graph showing the data from both experiments with temperature versus time.

(5) Draw and label two sketches, showing your apparatus for both experiments.

Figure 4.4. Graph Title for Procedure #4

Lab Meteorology 4: (M-4) Sweating About Science

Part 1: (Teacher's Lesson Plan Outline)

Note: See Lesson Planning on page 32.

Anticipation Section Title: (M-4) Sweating About Science

Problem: Is there a difference between indoor humidity and outdoor humidity?

Prediction: Give a working definition of *relative humidity*.

Thinking About the Problem: (See p. 170.)

Data Collection Materials and Procedures: (See p. 171.)

Expansion and Further Investigation:

(1) Research the relative humidity of Colorado Springs, Colorado, and Phoenix, Arizona, during the past 20 years. How does construction of residential areas, landscaping around businesses, and city development affect or influence relative humidity?

(2) Some people's hair curls when the relative humidity is high. Think of a way to use this fact to measure relative humidity. Include a labeled sketch of the device you would use with your explanation.

Part 2: (Student Lab Notebook Entries)

Anticipation Section Title: (M-4) Sweating About Science

Problem: Is there a difference between indoor humidity and outdoor humidity?

Prediction:

Note: Distribute the student handout (see *Part 3*) after students have completed their predictions.

Thinking About the Problem: Paraphrase the three main points of the reading in your own words.

(1)

(2)

(3)

Table 4.9. Data Collection Table #1: Relative Humidity Data

Location	Time	Dry Bulb Temp (°C)	Wet Bulb Temp (°C)	Difference (°C)	Relative Humidity (%)

Analysis:

(1) What did you notice about the wet bulb temperature while you were swinging the sling psychrometer (p. 171)?

(2) Give a good explanation for what you observed in question #1 above.

(3) Was there a difference between the indoor and outdoor relative humidity? Explain.

Concluding-the-Analysis Statements:

(1) I learned…

(2) If I were to re-do this lab, I would change…

(3) An example of a variable in this lab is…

(4) An example of a control in this lab is…

Table 4.10. Data Collection Table #2: Percentage of Relative Humidity

Difference (°C)	Dry Bulb Temp (°C) 5	6	7	8	9	10	11	12	13	14	15	16	17	18	19	20	21	22	23	24	25	26	27	28	29	30	31	32	33	34	35
1	86	86	87	87	88	88	89	89	90	90	90	90	90	91	91	91	92	92	92	92	92	92	92	93	93	93	93	93	93	93	94
2	72	73	74	75	76	77	78	78	79	79	80	81	81	82	82	83	83	83	84	84	84	85	85	85	86	86	86	86	87	87	87
3	58	60	62	63	64	66	67	68	69	70	71	71	72	73	74	74	75	76	76	77	77	78	78	78	79	79	80	80	80	81	81
4	45	48	50	51	53	55	56	58	59	60	61	63	64	65	65	66	67	68	69	69	70	71	71	72	72	73	73	74	74	75	75
5	33	35	38	40	42	44	46	48	50	51	53	54	55	57	58	59	60	61	62	62	63	64	65	65	66	67	67	68	68	69	69
6	20	24	26	29	32	34	36	39	41	42	44	46	47	49	50	51	53	54	55	56	57	58	58	59	60	61	61	62	63	63	64
7	7	11	15	19	22	24	27	29	32	34	36	38	40	41	43	44	46	47	48	49	50	51	52	53	54	55	56	57	57	58	59
8				8	12	15	18	21	23	26	27	30	32	34	36	37	39	40	42	43	44	46	47	48	49	50	51	51	52	53	54
9						6	9	12	15	18	20	23	25	27	29	31	32	34	36	37	39	40	41	42	43	44	45	46	47	48	49
10									7	10	13	15	18	20	22	24	26	28	30	31	33	34	36	37	38	39	40	41	42	43	44
11											6	8	11	14	16	18	20	22	24	26	28	29	31	32	33	35	36	37	38	39	40
12														7	10	12	14	17	19	20	22	24	26	27	28	30	31	32	33	35	36

Part 3: (Student Handout)

Note: Distribute to students after they complete the Prediction in *Part 2.*

Anticipation Section Title: (M-4) Sweating About Science

Thinking About the Problem

Why do we seem to perspire more when it is humid? This is actually a misconception that many people share. The truth has to do with evaporation. In dry air, it is easier for water to evaporate and enter the air as water vapor. On very humid days, the air is already holding as much water vapor as it can, so perspiration is unable to evaporate as easily. The perspiration sits on our skin, rather than evaporating off, as it does on a dry day.

Hot, dry air is normally more comfortable than warm, humid air. Similarly, cold, dry air is often more comfortable than cool, damp air. While there is always at least a small amount of moisture in the air we breathe, the amount makes a big difference on our comfort level. Why? Temperature plays the primary role in determining the amount of water vapor present in the air at any given time. Warm air can hold more water vapor than cool air. But every temperature has its limit and once the air is saturated, it can hold no more water vapor. Saturated air has a relative humidity of 100% and clouds or fog begin to form. When relative humidity is high, our perspiration cannot evaporate quickly, it is much harder for us to cool down, and we become uncomfortable.

Relative humidity is a measure of how much water vapor is actually in the air compared to the amount the air could possibly hold. In desert areas, relative humidity is low, but in jungles it is high. Relative humidity can be measured with two different instruments. One is called a hygrometer (*hugros*, "wet, moist" in Greek); the other is called a sling psychrometer (*psukhros*, "cold" in Greek). Since the sling psychrometer is easily portable, that is the one we will use in this lab.

Data Collection Materials:

- Data Table: Percentage of Relative Humidity

- Sling psychrometer

- Thermometer

Data Collection Procedures:

(1) Read and record the "dry bulb temperature" on the metal thermometer.

(2) Carefully swing the sling psychrometer around for two to three minutes and record the lowest temperature reached by its thermometer. Record this "wet bulb temperature."

(3) Subtract the wet bulb temperature from the dry bulb temperature, and record.

(4) From your calculation in step 3, determine the relative humidity using Data Collection Table #2.

(5) Use this same method to determine the relative humidity in four more locations around the school.

$SC{}^{\bullet}_{LINKS}$
THE WORLD'S A CLICK AWAY

Topic: Weather Patterns

Go to: *www.scilinks.org*

Code: ESS029

$SC{}^{\bullet}_{LINKS}$
THE WORLD'S A CLICK AWAY

Topic: Air Masses and Fronts

Go to: *www.scilinks.org*

Code: ESS030

Lab Meteorology 5: (M-5) Lining Up in Front

Part 1: (Teacher's Lesson Plan Outline)

Note: See Lesson Planning on page 32.

Anticipation Section Title: (M-5) Lining Up in Front

Problem: How do warm and cold fronts influence the weather you see?

Prediction: Answer the problem question above.

Thinking About the Problem: (See p. 176.)

Data Collection Materials and Procedures: (See p. 177.)

Expansion and Further Investigation:

(1) Research the four different types of clouds and the type of weather that is generally associated with each. Write a detailed half-page report on your findings. Include pictures or diagrams of each type.

(2) Research and report on the weather proverb, "Mackerel skies and mares tales make tall ships carry low sails." What does the proverb mean, and exactly what would the cloud conditions be if it was applicable?

(3) Research "cloud in a jar" demonstrations on the internet. Using the simple materials required, prepare a demonstration for the class in which you generate a cloud in a jar.

Part 2: (Student Lab Notebook Entries)

Anticipation Section Title: (M-5) Lining Up in Front

Problem: How do warm and cold fronts influence the weather you see?

Prediction:

Note: Distribute the student handout (see *Part 3*) after students have completed their prediction.

Thinking About the Problem: Paraphrase the three main points of the reading in your own words.

(1)

(2)

(3)

Figure 4.5. Data Collection Table #1: Front Lines Data Page

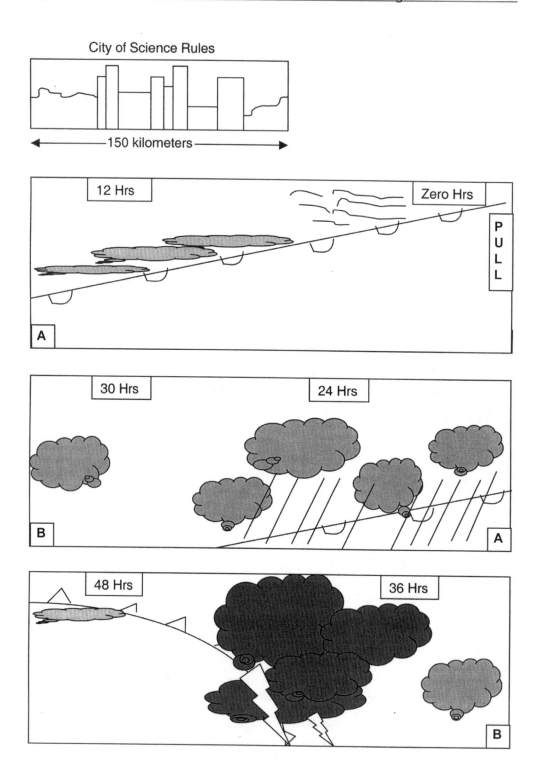

Analysis:

(1) Describe what the clouds looked like during the first few hours.

(2) What did the clouds look like after 24 hours, when it was raining?

(3) Why did the warm air mass rise up over the cold air mass?

(4) Describe the types of clouds present as the cold front moved into the city after 48 hours.

(5) If you saw wispy clouds followed by lower, layered clouds, what type of weather might you expect in the next 24 hours?

Concluding-the-Analysis Statements:

(1) I learned…

(2) If I were to re-do this lab, I would change…

(3) An example of a variable in this lab is…

(4) An example of a control in this lab is…

Part 3: (Student Handout)

Note: Distribute to students after they complete the Prediction in *Part 2*.

Anticipation Section Title: (M-5) Lining Up in Front

Thinking About the Problem

What is a weather front? When a warm air mass meets a cool air mass, two distinct bodies of air are brought in contact, each with its own temperature and relative humidity. Normally, when this "collision" happens, the warm air mass rides up and over the cool air mass, because warm air is less dense. A front is, then, the boundary, or line, between these two air masses.

When a weather front results in warm air getting pushed above cool air, the warm air mass swells as it goes higher and higher. This happens because the air pressure is lower at higher altitudes. As the warm air rises and expands, it begins to cool and the moisture it contains condenses to form clouds and, often, rain, ice, or snow. Clouds come in different shapes and sizes and this is a factor that meteorologists use to help predict the weather.

Dew is the result of air reaching a certain temperature at which it becomes saturated. As you learned in Lab M-4, saturation occurs when the air can hold no more water vapor. This vapor will begin to change to liquid, as, for example, often happens in early morning when moist air condenses on cooler grass, rocks, and trees. If the temperature of the grass, etc., is below freezing, the condensation (*densare*, "to thicken" in Latin) is known as frost. The temperature at which the processes of evaporation and condensation are equal is called the dew point.

Data Collection Materials:

- Front lines data page (Figure 4.5)

- Glue

- Notebook paper

- Scissors

Data Collection Procedures:

(1) Find the data page. Separate the three strips, cutting along the lines. Also cut out the "city" (the smaller box on top).

(2) Shade in the cold air masses, so they are easier for you to see.

(3) Glue the three strips together by matching up the letters.

(4) To make the viewer, fold a piece of notebook paper in half and make two 6 cm cuts that are vertical, as shown in Figure 4.6.

Figure 4.6. Frame for Viewer

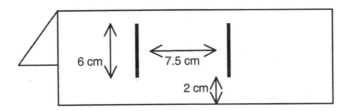

(5) Glue the city below the two cuts.

(6) Feed the strip through the two cuts so that it passes over the city, starting with Zero Hrs.

Lab Meteorology 6: (M-6) Dewing Science

Part 1: (Teacher's Lesson Plan Outline)

Note: See Lesson Planning on page 32.

Anticipation Section Title: (M-6) Dewing Science

Problem: How does the dew point of our air influence us?

Prediction: Give a working definition of *dew point*.

Thinking About the Problem: (See p. 181.)

Data Collection Materials and Procedures: (See p. 182.)

Note: You may want to conduct this experiment outside if you teach in an air-conditioned building.

Expansion and Further Investigation:

(1) When air rises, it expands and cools about 1°C for every 100 m of altitude, up to about 10 km. If the air in our classroom were to rise, at what height would the water vapor begin to condense and form clouds? Explain your answer. (Assume that the air outside has the same temperature as inside.)

(2) At what time of day are you most likely to find dew? Why? Where would you normally find dew? Describe the situations when you might find frozen dew.

Part 2: (Student Lab Notebook Entries)

Anticipation Section Title: (M-6) Dewing Science

Problem: How does the dew point of our air influence us?

Prediction:

Note: Distribute the student handout (see *Part 3*) after students have completed their predictions.

Thinking About the Problem: Paraphrase the three main points of the reading in your own words.

(1)

(2)

(3)

Table 4.11. Data Collection Table #1: Dewing Science Experiments

Trial	Air Temp. (°C)	Dew Point (°C)	Descriptive Observations
1			
2			
3			
Average Dew Point (°C)			

Analysis:

(1) Under what weather conditions would both the air temperature and the dew point be the same number?

(2) Imagine that you are doing this activity again, on a day with similar air temperature. If you found that the dew point had increased, would this indicate that there was more moisture in the air, or less? Explain.

(3) By how many degrees would the air temperature have to cool in order to reach the average dew point determined in Data Collection Table #1? Explain.

Concluding-the-Analysis Statements:

(1) I learned...

(2) If I were to re-do this lab, I would change...

(3) An example of a variable in this lab is...

(4) An example of a control in this lab is...

Part 3: (Student Handout)

Note: Distribute to students after they complete the Prediction in *Part 2*.

Anticipation Section Title: (M-6) Dewing Science

Thinking About the Problem

Can the dew point influence how we feel? On muggy days, meteorologists often include the dew point in the facts and figures that they share. Why? The answer is that the dew point is a good indication of how much moisture (invisible water vapor gas) is in the air. The closer the dew point is to the actual air temperature, the more moisture the air is holding. We are most likely to notice water vapor on very humid, warm days, when we feel clammy or sticky because, as you learned in Lab M-4, all the water vapor surrounding us prevents our perspiration from evaporating easily.

On days when the air temperature and the dew point are very close to each other, we say the air is "humid." If, for example, the air temperature is 31°C and the dew point is 29°C, this means that there is much more water vapor in the air than on a day when the temperature is the same but the dew point is only 10°C.

As you learned in Lab M-1, most of the water in the atmosphere got there by evaporation, largely from the ocean but also from lakes, rivers, ponds, and even puddles. Temperature is a major factor in determining how much and how rapidly water will evaporate from these places. When the air is cool, it cannot hold as much water vapor as when the air is warm, and therefore, less water will evaporate. Because of this, at any location, there will probably be more water vapor in the air during warm weather than during cold weather. In this lab, you will investigate the relationship between air temperature and dew point.

Data Collection Materials:

- Empty soup can

- Ice

- Metal thermometer

- Water

Data Collection Procedures:

(1) Measure and record the air temperature.

(2) Fill the can half full with water. Allow the can to sit for three minutes. If condensation forms on the outside of the can, replace the water with slightly warmer water. Repeat until no condensation forms on the outside of the can.

(3) Place the thermometer in the can with the water.

(4) Slowly, add small pieces of ice to the can while carefully stirring with the thermometer. Watch the outside of the can for the first sign of condensation.

(5) When condensation begins, immediately record the "dew point" temperature of the water in the can.

(6) Repeat steps 2 through 5 twice more and record. Find the average and record.

Lab Meteorology 7: (M-7) Deciphering a Weather Map

Part 1: (Teacher's Lesson Plan Outline)

Note: See Lesson Planning on page 32.

Anticipation Section Title: (M-7) Deciphering a Weather Map

Problem: What do all the symbols mean on a standard weather map?

Prediction: Describe what types of information a weather station collects.

Thinking About the Problem: (See p. 189.)

Data Collection Materials and Procedures: (See p. 189.)

Notes on Weather Symbol Information:

(1) **Atmospheric Pressure:** This is the air pressure measured in millibars (mb). Average air pressure at sea level is 1013 mb. This is equivalent to 760 mm Hg (Metric Standard) and to 29.92 in Hg (used by some meteorologists). On the weather map, "056" refers to 1005.6 mb.

(2) **Wind Speed:** Small lines represent the wind speed. Each full line represents 10 knots (1 kt = 1.15 mph). Shorter lines represent 5 knots. Add the lines to get the total wind speed.

(3) **Wind Direction:** The line points in the direction from which the wind is blowing. For example, wind is blowing "from the south" for the city of Science Rules.

(4) **Temperature:** Temperature is measured in °F.

(5) **Dew Point:** This is the temperature, in °F, that the air would have to be cooled down to in order for the air to become saturated and condense. In other words, the closer the dew point is to the actual temperature, the more humid it feels.

(6) **Cloud Cover:** The amount of cloud cover is represented by the amount of the circle that is darkened.

(7) **Precipitation:** These symbols show the current type and level of precipitation.

Expansion and Further Investigation:

(1) Why is it important to be informed about weather conditions? Describe 10 careers that rely on forecasted weather conditions.

(2) Describe any weather conditions that could occur in your community that pose threats to life and/or property.

SC*I*INKS.
THE WORLD'S A CLICK AWAY

Topic: Weather Maps
Go to: *www.scilinks.org*
Code: ESS031

Part 2: (Student Lab Notebook Entries)

Anticipation Section Title: (M-7) Deciphering a Weather Map

Problem: What do all the symbols mean on a weather map?

Prediction:

Note: Distribute the student handout (see *Part 3*) after students have completed their predictions.

Thinking About the Problem: Paraphrase the three main points of the reading in your own words.

(1)

(2)

(3)

Table 4.12. Sketch for Analysis #14

Figure 4.7. Data Collection Table #1: Weather Station Symbol

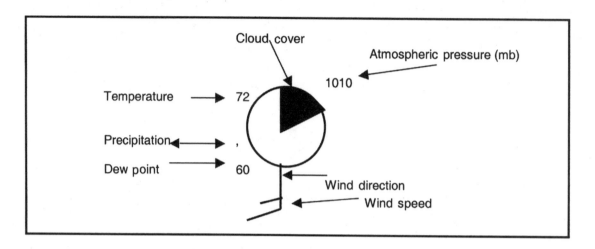

Figure 4.8. Data Collection Table #2: Weather Symbols for Wind Speeds

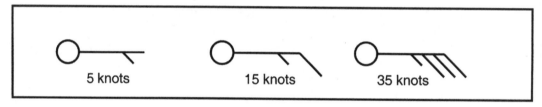

Figure 4.9. Data Collection Table #3: Weather Symbols for Wind Direction

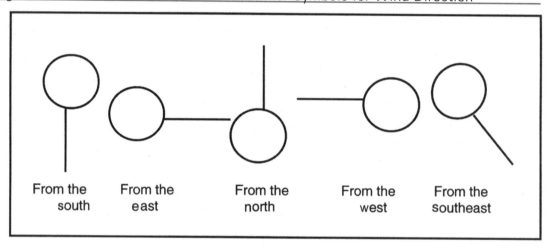

Figure 4.10. Data Collection Table #4: Weather Symbols for Cloud Cover

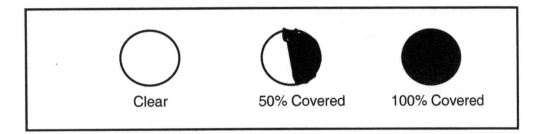

Clear	50% Covered	100% Covered

Table 4.13. Data Collection Table #5: Weather Station Symbols for Precipitation

Symbol	Precipitation	Symbol	Precipitation
•	Intermittent rain	'	Intermittent drizzle
• •	Continuous rain	' '	Continuous drizzle
Δ	Hail	⟋⧏	Thunderstorms
Δ•	Sleet	' =	Fog
*	Intermittent snow	▽	Slight showers
* *	Continuous snow	▽	Heavy showers

Analysis:

(1) What is the current precipitation in Pueblo, Colorado?

(2) What is the atmospheric pressure in Miami, Florida?

(3) Describe the wind direction and wind speed in Winnipeg, Manitoba.

(4) What is the temperature in San Antonio, Texas?

(5) What is the cloud cover in Boston, Massachusetts?

(6) What is the atmospheric pressure in Phoenix, Arizona?

(7) What is the precipitation in Chicago, Illinois?

(8) What is the cloud cover in Seattle, Washington?

(9) Describe the wind direction and wind speed in Los Angeles, California.

(10) Describe the precipitation in Minneapolis, Minnesota.

(11) Describe the region of the map that appears to be generally cloudy.

(12) Describe the region of the map that appears to be generally clear.

(13) Describe a region in the map that fits your ideal weather, and explain why.

(14) In the city Science Rules, the weather has changed to the following conditions: atmospheric pressure is 1015 mb; temperature is 54°F; dew point is 40°F; wind is 25 knots from the southeast; and cloud cover is 50%. Draw and label the current weather symbol for Science Rules.

Concluding-the-Analysis Statements:

(1) I learned…

(2) If I were to re-do this lab, I would change…

(3) An example of a variable in this lab is…

(4) An example of a control in this lab is…

Part 3: (Student Handout)

Note: Distribute to students after they complete the Prediction in *Part 2.*

Anticipation Section Title: (M-7) Deciphering a Weather Map

Thinking About the Problem

What do we need to know to interpret weather maps? These maps report meteorological data collected from several weather stations at a specific point in time. Weather stations can be in many places, including airports, TV and radio broadcasting stations, schools, private homes, and remote areas maintained by the National Oceanic and Atmospheric Administration (NOAA).

Normally weather maps show an outline of a specific area (local, state, national), the cities where the reporting stations are located, and symbols to show what the weather is. By including information from a number of different stations, the map will give a good idea of what the weather is across the whole area represented.

Data Collection Table #1 shows an example of a weather station's symbol and the information given by each part of the symbol. Although this current system may change, weather station symbols in the United States are still expressed with the English Standard units of measurement, rather than the metric system. Data Collection Tables #2, #3, #4, and #5 show examples of specific information presented by weather station symbols.

Data Collection Materials:

- Data collection tables of weather station symbols (Figures 4.7–4.10; 4.12)

- Weather map (Figure 4.11)

Data Collection Procedures:

(1) Refer to the data collection tables and to the weather map in answering the Analysis questions.

Figure 4.11. Weather Map

Figure 4.12. Weather Station Symbols for Each City on the National Map

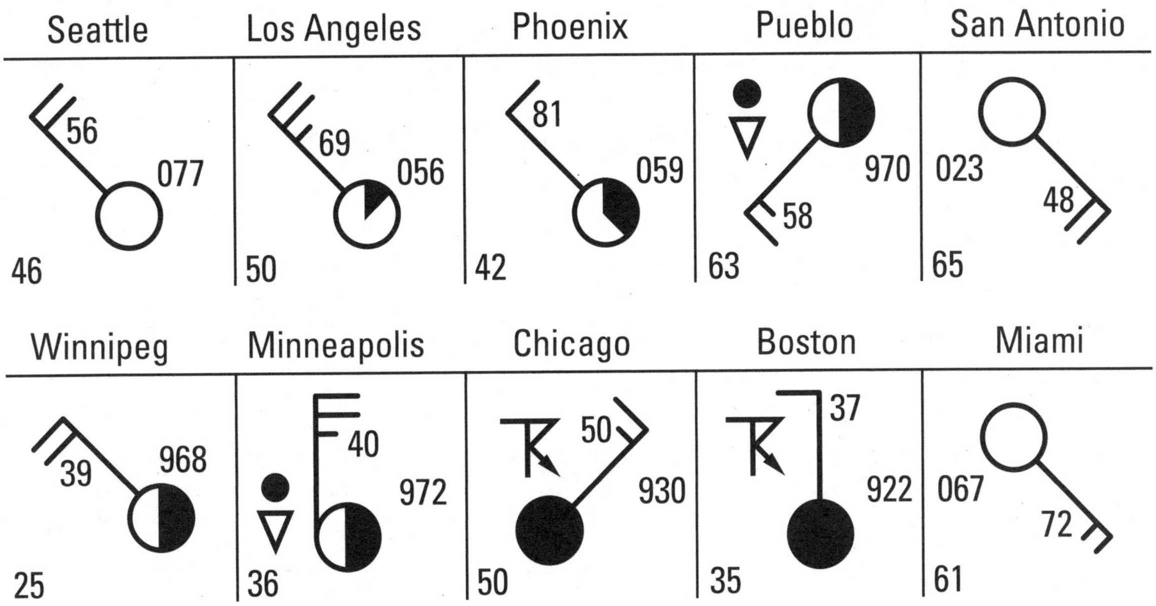

Lab Meteorology 8: (M-8) Watching the Weather

Part 1: (Teacher's Lesson Plan Outline)

Note: See Lesson Planning on page 32.

Anticipation Section Title: (M-8) Watching the Weather

Problem: What is the connection between North American and your local weather patterns?

Prediction: Describe, in one sentence, your answer to the problem question.

Thinking About the Problem: (See p. 197.)

Data Collection Materials and Procedures: (See p. 198.)

Note: You may want to make copies of the Watching the Weather data sheet for students to glue into their lab notebooks. I select the cities to record daily high temperature and precipitation forecasts. This gives a good idea to students about where the air masses that might be affecting their hometown are coming from. The daily newspaper can be used to obtain this information, in addition to numerous online sources. We have a WeatherBug Weather Station in our classroom for use with all of the rest of the daily data. You can access weather stations such as this through *www.weatherbug.com*.

Expansion and Further Investigation:

(1) Describe, in a detailed half-page report, what the connection is between front movements and the precipitation that comes to your area.

(2) Research South American, European, African, or Asian weather patterns and report on how they are similar to, and different from, your own weather patterns.

SC*L*INKS.
THE WORLD'S A CLICK AWAY

Topic: Weather Forecasting

Go to: *www.scilinks.org*

Code: ESS032

Part 2: (Student Lab Notebook Entries)

Anticipation Section Title: (M-8) Watching the Weather

Problem: What is the connection between North American and your local weather patterns?

Prediction:

Note: Distribute the student handout (see *Part 3*) after students have completed their predictions.

Thinking About the Problem: Paraphrase the three main points of the reading in your own words.

(1)

(2)

(3)

Table 4.14. Data Collection Table #1: Watching the Weather

Today's Day and Date: _____

Watching the Weather	
Cloud types	Morning: Noon: Evening:
Precipitation	Type: Total amount: Duration:
Temperature	High: Temp at noon: Low:
Air pressure	Morning: Noon: Evening:

Analysis:

(1) Find one of your Watching the Weather data sheets that shows some form of precipitation. Describe the kinds of clouds you observed on that day.

(2) On that same day, look at the North American weather map. Where in the continent were the major fronts and what types of fronts were they?

(3) Follow the movements of a front to see how it moves each day. Describe the direction in which it moved.

(4) What is the general direction of weather movement over North America?

(5) If you could spend a lot of time watching the weather, where would you discover that most of your hometown's weather comes from?

Concluding-the-Analysis Statements:

(1) I learned…

(2) If I were to re-do this lab, I would change…

(3) An example of a variable in this lab is…

(4) An example of a control in this lab is…

Part 3: (Student Handout)

Note: Distribute to students after they complete the Prediction in *Part 2*.

Anticipation Section Title: (M-8) Watching the Weather

Thinking About the Problem

What is the weather like outside right now? Can you answer the question without looking out the window to check? What type of cloud cover was in the sky when you woke up this morning? If you have trouble answering these questions, you are not alone. Most people today do not pay very much attention to the weather until it interferes with something they plan to do. Rain can cancel a soccer game. Snow can make a commute unbearable. When these things happen we notice the weather, but much of the time we ignore it.

This is not the case, of course, for everyone. Receiving proper amounts of rain and sun is vital for those who grow the food we eat. Sailors, pilots, truck drivers, and a number of other professions depend on accurate weather reports to be able to safely carry out the work they do. "Red sky at night, sailor's delight; red sky in the morning, sailors take warning" is only one of the many sayings in our language that prove that our ancestors were very concerned with the weather and that they knew how to read natural signs in order to predict what the weather would be.

By not paying attention, we miss many of the interesting things that go on in the atmosphere. For example, it is possible to predict short-term weather changes with some accuracy just by looking at the clouds. The purpose of this lab is to help you observe the weather around you more carefully and to help you relate the weather you're experiencing to weather in other parts of the country. One way to predict weather changes is to look at the weather in nearby places. You can become an excellent forecaster by carefully observing what is happening around you.

Data Collection Materials:

- Classroom weather station

- Internet sites for monitoring current and forecasted weather

- North American weather maps from local newspapers

- Watching the Weather data collection tables (4.14)

Data Collection Procedures:

(1) Create one Watching the Weather data collection table for each day, for 10 days total. Glue in the 10 North American maps and draw one data table beneath them per page.

(2) Record the information from the internet/newspaper weather maps onto your weather map data sheet each day. Include the temperatures in major cities across North America, as well as the various types and locations of fronts.

(3) Record the daily weather conditions at your location.

Chapter 5

Physical Oceanography

Note to the teacher: Students investigate the unique properties of water and how these properties shape the ocean and the entire planet. Students perform activities investigating the complex systems that lead to the development of currents, waves, and tides. Students focus on the interaction of wind, water, gravity, buoyancy, density, pressure, and inertia.

We believe that Labs O-4 through O-8 are examples of authentic scaffolding for understanding the abstract concept of density. Each of these labs builds on the one that precedes it and adds new depth to the concept.

There are five main misconceptions held by some students that get defeated by these labs:

(1) All bigger or heavier things will sink.

(2) All smaller or lighter things will float.

(3) Larger amounts of water make things float.

(4) Hollow things float.

(5) Things with holes will sink. (Yin 2005)[1]

The 10-day outline in Table 5.1, assumes that your course started with the Earth Systems Science Pretest, Lab S-1, and the astronomy unit. If, however, you choose to cover Physical Oceanography first, we recommend that you still begin with the Pretest and Lab S-1 (see Chapter 1, "The First Ten Days").

Table 5.1. Possible Syllabus for the First Ten Days of Oceanography

	Day 1	Day 2	Day 3	Day 4	Day 5
Week 1	KWL flip book, Lab O-1 (anticipation)	Lab O-1 (data collection)	Lab O-1 (analysis)	Lab O-2 (anticipation)	Lab O-1 (report due), Lab O-2 (data collection)
Week 2	Lab O-2 (analysis)	Lab O-2 (finish analysis), Lab O-3 (anticipation)	Lab O-3 (data collection)	Lab O-2 (report due), Lab O-3 (analysis)	Lab O-4 (anticipation)

---

[1]Yin, Y. 2005. The influence of formative assessments on student motivation, achievement, and conceptual change. PhD dissertation, Stanford University.

Lab Oceanography 1: (O-1) Piling Up the Water

Part 1: (Teacher's Lesson Plan Outline)

Note: See Lesson Planning on page 32.

Anticipation Section Title: (O-1) Piling Up the Water

Problem: Which of the five containers will be able to withstand the addition of the greatest number of pennies without spilling over?

Prediction: Describe, in one sentence, which container you choose and why.

Thinking About the Problem: (See p. 205.)

Data Collection Materials and Procedures: (See p. 206.)

Safety Requirements: goggles, aprons

Expansion and Further Investigation:

(1) Compare the surface tension of tap water and saltwater. Although the addition of impurities—like salt—decreases the cohesion between water molecules, it also increases the density of water (allowing things to float more easily). Sketch and record your results.

(2) Research and write a detailed half-page report on either capillary action (the mechanism by which plants transport water from their roots throughout the plant) or "water striders" (animals that take advantage of water's surface tension to live on the surface of the water).

SC*LINKS*®
THE WORLD'S A CLICK AWAY

Topic: Properties of Water

Go to: *www.scilinks.org*

Code: ESS033

Part 2: (Student Lab Notebook Entries)

Anticipation Section Title: (O-1) Piling Up the Water

Problem: Which of the five containers will be able to withstand the addition of the greatest number of pennies without spilling over?

Prediction:

Note: Distribute the student handout (see *Part 3*) after students have completed their predictions.

Thinking About the Problem: Paraphrase the three main points of the reading in your own words.

    (1)

    (2)

    (3)

Table 5.2. Sketch for Procedure #5

Table 5.3. Data Collection Table #1: Data for Full Containers

Container #	Description	Predicted Pennies	Actual Pennies
1			
2			
3			
4			
5			

Table 5.4. Data Collection Table #2: Drops of Water on Coins

Coin	Predicted Drops	Actual Drops
Penny		
Nickel		
Dime		
Quarter		

Table 5.5. Data Collection Table #3: Drops of Soapy Water on Coins

Coin	Predicted Drops	Actual Drops
Penny		
Nickel		
Dime		
Quarter		

Analysis:

    (1) Describe the shape of the water as it "sits" on a coin.

    (2) Why does water pile up on a coin, rather than spill over the edges immediately? How is the soapy water different? (Describe the science behind your thoughts. Thinking About the Problem will help you here.)

    (3) Use science concepts to suggest reasons why each of the five containers holds a different number of pennies.

Concluding-the-Analysis Statements:

    (1) I learned…

    (2) If I were to re-do this lab, I would change…

    (3) An example of a variable in this lab is…

    (4) An example of a control in this lab is…

Part 3: (Student Handout)

Note: Distribute to students after they complete the Prediction in *Part 2.*

Anticipation Section Title: (O-1) Piling Up the Water

Thinking About the Problem

What does H_2O mean? As you learned in Lab M-1, each molecule (*molecula*, "small bit" in Latin) of water is made of two hydrogen atoms (H_2) and one oxygen atom (O). What is special about water molecules is that they tend to "stick" to each other (cohesion) and to other molecules (adhesion). They do this because water is built like a magnet, with a positive end and a negative end. This helps it bond well. During this lab, you will explore this bonding ability of water.

Water makes life on Earth possible. It covers almost three-fourths of the surface of our planet. Because there is so much of it, water may seem very ordinary to us, and yet it is unique when compared with all other substances. For example, water is the only substance on Earth that occurs naturally in all three states—solid, liquid, and gas. Solid H_2O (ice) is less dense than its liquid form (water) so it floats. Most other solids are denser than their liquid form, so they sink! Another difference, with respect to water, is that large amounts of energy must be added to water to achieve even a relatively small change in temperature.

Data Collection Materials:

- Beaker

- Dish soap

- Eyedropper

- Large water containers (assortment of five beakers, buckets, or bowls)

- Many pennies

- Other coins

Data Collection Procedures:

(1) Predict which of your five large containers (each full to the rim with water) will be able to withstand the addition of the greatest number of pennies without spilling over. Test and record your results.

(2) Place a dry penny on a piece of paper towel.

(3) Predict the number of drops you can pile on the penny before water runs over the edge.

(4) Test and record for each particular coin.

(5) Draw and label a sketch of the water on the surface of the coin just before the water spilled over.

(6) Conduct the same tests with the soapy water.

SC*i*LINKS®
THE WORLD'S A CLICK AWAY

Topic: Properties of Ocean Water

Go to: *www.scilinks.org*

Code: ESS034

Lab Oceanography 2: (O-2) Layering Around on the Beach

Part 1: (Teacher's Lesson Plan Outline)

Note: See Lesson Planning on page 32.

Anticipation Section Title: (O-2) Layering Around on the Beach

Problem: What happens when ocean water, brackish water, and river water contact one another?

Prediction: Describe, in one sentence, your answer to the problem question.

Thinking About the Problem: (See p. 210.)

Data Collection Materials and Procedures: (See p. 211.)

Safety requirements: goggles

Expansion and Further Investigation:

(1) New research into global warming shows that the melting of the polar ice caps is affecting the level of salts in the northern oceans. Research this idea further, and write a detailed half-page report on how this might affect sea life.

(2) Suppose you are at the seacoast in an area where a river runs into a somewhat salty bay before it reaches the ocean. Where do you predict that you would find the saltiest water: near the surface of the bay or near its bottom? Explain why.

Part 2: (Student Lab Notebook Entries)

Anticipation Section Title: (O-2) Layering Around on the Beach

Problem: What happens when ocean water, brackish water, and river water contact one another?

Prediction:

Note: Distribute the student handout (see *Part 3*) after students have completed their predictions.

Thinking About the Problem: Paraphrase the three main points of the reading in your own words.

   (1)

   (2)

   (3)

Table 5.6. Sketch for Procedure #7

Table 5.7. Data Collection Table #1: Data on Beach Investigation

Hypothesis #1: Observation:
Hypothesis #2: Observation:
Hypothesis #3 Observation:
Hypothesis #4: Observation:

Analysis:

    (1) Explain how you were able to develop different ocean layers.

    (2) What happens when ocean water, brackish water, and river water contact one another?

Concluding-the-Analysis Statements:

    (1) I learned…

    (2) If I were to re-do this lab, I would change…

    (3) An example of a variable in this lab is…

    (4) An example of a control in this lab is…

Part 3: (Student Handout)

Note: Distribute to students after they complete the Prediction in *Part 2*.

Anticipation Section Title: (O-2) Layering Around on the Beach

---

Thinking About the Problem

What makes the water in the sea different from the water in a river? Water has different properties depending on the environment in which it is found. We call water in the ocean saltwater because it has a lot of salts dissolved in it. Water in streams and rivers is called freshwater because it does not contain many dissolved salts. When rivers flow into the ocean, the mouth of the river is called an estuary (*aestus*, "tidal surge" in Latin). Water in an estuary is "brackish," meaning it has a higher amount of salts than freshwater but a lower amount than the open ocean.

Ocean water is not the same everywhere. In some places the water is colder or deeper than in others. Some bodies of water are denser or contain differing amounts of dissolved salts than others. All of these factors influence the way ocean water behaves.

Although water is the most abundant substance on Earth's surface, very little of it is pure. In addition to hydrogen and oxygen—the only two elements in pure water—there are many other elements mixed in with the water on our planet. Tap water, for example, contains chemicals used to disinfect the water and prevent bacterial growth.

In this lab we will explore how different types of water—salt, brackish, and fresh—form layers and mix. This will help us to understand the effects that this "layering around on the beach" has on Earth's environment.

Data Collection Materials:

- Three 250 mL beakers

- Three colored solutions

- Three eyedroppers

- Clear straw

- Small block of clay

- Waste container

Data Collection Procedures:

(1) Stick the straw into the clay at an angle, so there are no leaks.

(2) You know only the following two facts about your solutions:

- The only difference between the solutions is their color and the amount of salt they contain.

- If you add small amounts of each solution to the straw in the correct order, you will produce three distinct layers that do not mix.

(3) Your goal is to determine which colors correspond to salt, fresh, and brackish water.

(4) Make a hypothesis in Data Collection Table #1.

(5) Test your hypothesis by adding a small amount of each solution to the straw in the order that you guessed. Record your observations in Data Collection Table #1.

(6) If you did not see three distinct layers, revise your hypothesis. Empty the contents of your straw into the waste container, and test the new hypothesis. Record your observations in Data Collection Table #1.

(7) Draw and label a sketch, showing your final layered results.

*SCi*LINKS.
THE WORLD'S A CLICK AWAY

Topic: Tides
Go to: *www.scilinks.org*
Code: ESS035

Lab Oceanography 3: (O-3) Changing Lunar Tides

Part 1: (Teacher's Lesson Plan Outline)

Note: See Lesson Planning on page 32.

Anticipation Section Title: (O-3) Changing Lunar Tides

Problem: What is the pattern or rhythm involved in tides?

Prediction: Describe, in one sentence, the answer to the problem question.

Thinking About the Problem: (See p. 217.)

Data Collection Materials and Procedures: (See p. 218.)

Expansion and Further Investigation:

(1) Long Island Sound, between New York and Connecticut, is surrounded by shallow sandbars, which prevent even small sailboats from coming close to shore at low tide without being grounded. But at high tide, these sandbars do not cause a problem for boats. On Day 10, the crew of a sailboat wants to get as close as possible to shore, without getting stuck in the sandbars. They radio you at the Coast Guard station to ask what time they should come in so as to take advantage of high tide and daylight. What should you tell them (use nonmilitary time)?

(2) You are staying at a beach house. At high tide, the water completely covers the part of the beach that is usable. On Day 6, you go out on the beach at 10:00 AM to read a book. After an hour the sound of the waves lulls you to sleep. How long can you sleep before you must either wake up or get wet? Explain how you figured this out.

Part 2: (Student Lab Notebook Entries)

Anticipation Section Title: (O-3) Changing Lunar Tides

Problem: What is the pattern or rhythm involved in tides?

Prediction:

Note: Distribute the student handout (see *Part 3*) after students have completed their predictions.

Thinking About the Problem: Paraphrase the three main points of the reading in your own words.

   (1)

   (2)

   (3)

Table 5.8. Data Collection Table #1: Tide Chart for Milford, Connecticut

Day	Times	Sea Level (m)	Day	Times	Sea Level (m)
1 ◑	A. 0523 B. 1130 C. 1752 D. 2351	A. 0.9 B. 3.7 C. 0.9 D. 4.0	16	C. 0657 D. 1115 A. 1832 B. 0031	C. 0.8 D. 3.6 A. 0.9 B. 3.8
2	A. 0601 B. 1247 C. 1807 D. 2345	A. 0.8 B. 3.7 C. 0.9 D. 3.9	17	C. 0647 D. 1254 A. 1942	C. 0.7 D. 3.7 A. 0.8
3	A. 0647 B. 1203 C. 1807 D. 2359	A. 0.8 B. 3.6 C. 0.9 D. 3.8	18	B. 0140 C. 0705 D. 1638 A. 2052	B. 3.7 C. 0.7 D. 3.8 A. 0.5
4	A. 0728 B. 1316 C. 1905	A. 0.8 B. 3.7 C. 1.0	19	B. 0240 C. 0834 D. 1454 A. 2123	B. 3.8 C. 0.7 D. 3.9 A. 0.6
5	D. 0003 A. 0831 B. 1407 C. 2005	D. 3.7 A. 0.7 B. 3.8 C. 0.5	20	B. 0340 C. 0953 D. 1534 A. 2253	B. 3.5 C. 0.8 D. 3.9 A. 0.6
6	D. 0232 A. 0920 B. 1530 C. 2115	D. 3.8 A. 0.7 B. 3.9 C. 0.6	21	B. 0220 C. 1037 D. 1614 A. 2313	B. 3.8 C. 0.7 D. 3.9 A. 0.6
7	D. 0322 A. 0945 B. 1558 C. 2245	D. 3.7 A. 0.7 B. 3.8 C. 0.5	22 ●	B. 0458 C. 1138 D. 1723 A. 0052	B. 4.1 C. 0.7 D. 4.0 A. 0.7
8 ○	D. 0412 A. 1049 B. 1645 C. 2333	D.3.5 A. 0.4 B. 3.9 C. 0.5	23	B. 0505 C. 1239 D. 1802	B. 3.5 C. 0.8 D. 3.9
9	D. 0536 A. 1154 B. 1705	D. 3.8 A. 0.7 B. 3.9	24	A. 0140 B. 0633 C. 1235 D. 1940	A. 0.8 B. 3.6 C. 0.9 D. 3.8

10	C. 0025	C. 0.8		25	A. 0159	A. 0.7
	D. 0636	D. 3.7			B. 0732	B. 3.7
	A. 1204	A. 0.9			C. 1343	C. 0.8
	B. 1844	B. 3.9			D. 1956	D. 4.0
11	C. 0137	C. 0.8		26	A. 0249	A. 0.8
	D. 0751	D. 3.6			B. 0850	B. 3.7
	A. 1353	A. 0.9			C. 1432	C. 0.9
	B. 1924	B. 3.8			D. 2042	D. 3.9
12	C. 0214	C. 0.8		27	A. 0351	A. 0.7
	D. 0801	D. 3.6			B. 0854	B. 3.7
	A. 1413	A. 0.9			C. 1530	C. 0.8
	B. 2136	B. 3.8			D. 2110	D. 4.0
13	C. 0322	C. 0.7		28	A. 0345	A. 0.8
	D. 0950	D. 3.7			B. 0952	B. 3.6
	A. 1547	A. 0.8			C. 1534	C. 0.9
	B. 2103	B. 4.0			D. 2153	D. 3.8
14	C. 0442	C. 0.8		29	A. 0429	A. 0.8
	D. 1000	D. 3.7			B. 1020	B. 3.4
	A. 1642	A. 0.9			C. 1642	C. 0.9
	B. 2232	B. 3.9			D. 2221	D. 3.5
15	C. 0551	C. 0.9		30	A. 0530	A. 0.7
	D. 1005	D. 3.6			B. 1004	B. 3.7
	A. 1732	A. 1.0			C. 1710	C. 0.8
	B. 2341	B. 3.8			D. 2254	D. 4.0

Analysis:

(1) About how much time passes between one low tide (A) and the next low tide (C)?

(2) About how much time passes between one high tide (B) and the next high tide (D)?

(3) When did the lowest low tide occur? When did the highest high tide occur?

(4) To which Moon phases did your two answers to #3 correspond?

(5) When did the highest low tide occur? When did the lowest high tide occur?

(6) To which Moon phases did your two answers to #5 correspond?

Concluding-the-Analysis Statements:

(1) I learned...

(2) If I were to re-do this lab, I would change...

(3) An example of a variable in this lab is...

(4) An example of a control in this lab is...

Part 3: (Student Handout)

Note: Distribute to students after they complete the Prediction in *Part 2.*

Anticipation Section Title: (O-3) Changing Lunar Tides

Thinking About the Problem

Have you ever spent time watching the tide come in or go out? Sitting on a beach and focusing on the tide helps us realize that there is a definite rhythm to the ocean. Sandbars may appear at low tide and rocks may be covered when the tide is high. The pattern repeats itself twice each day. Why?

Tides are the daily changes in ocean surface height caused by the powerful attraction between the Earth and the Moon. The Earth and the Moon are attracted to each other due to gravity (*gravis,* "heavy" in Latin). Since Earth has a much greater mass, the effect of the Earth's gravity is stronger. But the Moon does exert a strong gravitational force on Earth. This gravitational attraction leads to rhythmic rising and falling of the waterline along the beach. Since water is more easily moved than land, ocean water gets pulled over the land area that happens to be facing the Moon. This means the side of the Earth closest to the Moon will experience higher tides.

Tides are predictable changes in sea level that occur at regular intervals. There is a "high tide" when the sea level has risen to its highest point and a "low tide" when it falls to its lowest point. These tide changes affect humans in many ways. One of the impacts of tides is on ocean shipping. In many locations, ships can come to shore only at high tide. If they come in at low tide, they may be grounded.

Because tides affect us in so many ways, it is important to know when they will occur, and fortunately this can be predicted with accuracy. By making a graph of the tides and the sea level, you can see the pattern of changes over time. The data used in this activity is from the shore of a small island (Charles Island) off the coast of Milford, Connecticut, where the authors of this book spent many summers. It is located in Long Island Sound on the Atlantic Ocean, across from Port Jefferson, New York.

Data Collection Materials:

- Bright colored pencils
- Data sheets and graphing charts for Charles Island in Milford, Connecticut
- Glue
- Metric ruler
- Pencil
- Scissors

Data Collection Procedures:

(1) Locate the tide chart for Charles Island in Milford, Connecticut. Note that all times are in military (24-hour) time. For example, 0530 refers to 5:30 AM, and 1522 refers to 3:22 PM. An average of two low tides (A and C) and two high tides (B and D) occur each day.

(2) Number the horizontal axis so that you can fit 30 days worth of data across the bottom. The vertical axis will be height of sea level. Give the graph a descriptive title.

(3) Plot your data for Sea Level versus Time (in days) by first plotting all of the data for "A" (earliest low tide). Draw a line to connect all of the "A" points in the order that they were plotted.

(4) Repeat step 3 by plotting the data and drawing the lines for "B," "C," and "D." Use a different colored pencil for each line.

Figure 5.1. Graph Title: _____

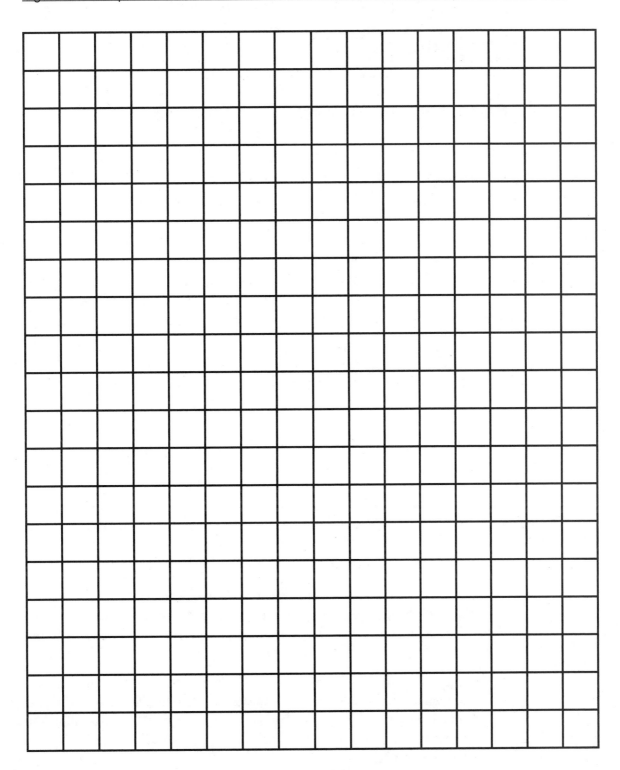

Lab Oceanography 4: (O-4) Sinking Film Canisters

Part 1: (Teacher's Lesson Plan Outline)

Note: See Lesson Planning on page 32.

Anticipation Section Title: (O-4) Sinking Film Canisters

Problem: How can you predict the quantity of pennies necessary to sink a film canister to any chosen depth in water?

Prediction: Describe, in one sentence, your definition of the word *buoyancy*.

Thinking About the Problem: (See p. 225.)

Data Collection Materials and Procedures: (See pp. 226, 228.)

Safety Requirements: goggles, aprons

*SCI*LINKS®
THE WORLD'S A CLICK AWAY

Topic: Buoyancy

Go to: *www.scilinks.org*

Code: ESS036

Expansion and Further Investigation:

(1) Suppose that the base diameter of one canister was twice as big as another canister. If both canisters, including their pennies, have the same mass, would they sink to the same depth? If you believe they would sink to the same depth, why? If not, why not?

(2) Extrapolate (predict beyond your range of data) to determine the quantity of pennies that would sink the canister to 4 cm. Explain how you found this. Interpolate (predict within your range of data) to determine the quantity of pennies that would sink the canister to 1.75 cm. Explain how you found this.

Part 2: (Student Lab Notebook Entries)

Anticipation Section Title: (O-4) Sinking Film Canisters

Problem: How can you predict the quantity of pennies necessary to sink a film canister to any chosen depth in water?

Prediction:

Note: Distribute the student handout (see *Part 3*) after students have completed their predictions.

Thinking About the Problem: Paraphrase the three main points of the reading in your own words.

(1)

(2)

(3)

Table 5.9. Data Collection Table #1: Data on Sinking a Film Canister

Length of Canister Below Rubber Band	Predicted Quantity of Pennies	Actual Quantity of Pennies
1 cm		
1.5 cm		
2 cm		
2.5 cm		

Table 5.10. Data Collection Table #2: Whole-Class Data on the Number of Pennies Needed to Sink the Canister to Each Depth

Lab Group	1 cm	1.5 cm	2 cm	2.5 cm		
A						
B						
C						
D						
E						
F						
G						
H						
I						
J						
K						
L						
M						
N						
O						

Table 5.11. Data Collection Table #3: Data on the Mass of Canister and Pennies

Length of Canister Below Surface	Average Quantity of Pennies	Prediction of Total Mass (g)	Actual Total Mass (g)
1 cm			
1.5 cm			
2 cm			
2.5 cm			

Table 5.12. Data Collection Table #4: Whole-Class Data on Mass of Canister and Pennies at Indicated Depths (g)

Lab Group	1 cm	1.5 cm	2 cm	2.5 cm		
A						
B						
C						
D						
E						
F						
G						
H						
I						
J						
K						
L						
M						
N						
O						

Analysis:

(1) Explain how you made your predictions for each event in Data Collection Tables #1 and #3.

(2) What kinds of instrument error could have affected the data collected?

(3) What kinds of human error could have affected the data collected?

(4) What properties of the pennies cause the canister to sink? Properties of objects are qualities we can observe or measure.

Use the Best Fit Line on your graph from *Part 1* to answer questions 5 and 6.

(5) How many pennies would it take to sink a canister 3.5 cm?

(6) How deep would a canister sink with three pennies?

Use the Best Fit Line on your graph from *Part 2* to answer question 7.

(7) What would the mass be of a canister that would sink 3 cm?

(8) What is the relationship between the total mass and the depth of sinking?

(9) How is your individual data similar to, and different from, the whole-class data?

(10) Describe what *mass* means, in your own words.

(11) Explain *buoyancy* in your own words.

Concluding-the-Analysis Statements:

(1) I learned…

(2) If I were to re-do this lab, I would change…

(3) An example of a variable in this lab is…

(4) An example of a control in this lab is…

Part 3: (Student Handout)

Note: Distribute to students after they complete the Prediction in *Part 2*.

Anticipation Section Title: (O-4) Sinking Film Canisters

Thinking About the Problem

How well do things float? To understand why something floats and how well, we need to understand *buoyancy*. Buoyancy is actually a result of the water pushing upward on objects. We will study buoyancy by experimenting with a floating film canister into which pennies can be placed.

For our investigation of buoyancy to be as accurate as possible, we need to isolate our variables and look at just one at a time. We will be sharing our data with the whole class to minimize errors. No measurement is exact and every measurement contains some uncertainty. Uncertainty in measurement is due partly to 1) instrument error because no instrument is perfect, and 2) human error because each person measures a little differently. One of the best ways to show all of the measurements is to make a graph.

A graph (*graphein*, "to write" in Greek) is a large picture of your data, which helps show regularities and patterns. From these patterns, we can predict events. For example, we can use the graph of the class data in *Part 1* of Lab O-4 to predict the quantity of pennies needed to sink a film canister to different depths. You will notice that the canister sinks a little, even with no pennies in it, so the pennies and the canister may have some similar property or properties. Remember that a property of an object is any quality that can be observed or measured. You will learn in Part 2 of Lab O-4 that both the canister and the pennies have the property of mass, which under the pull of gravity gives them weight. Mass is the measure of the physical bulk of an object (the amount of matter in it), simulated by the pennies in this lab.

Data Collection Materials:

- Pennies
- Metric ruler
- Triple beam balance
- Water

- Beakers
- Film canisters
- Graph paper

Procedures for Part 1:

(1) Move the rubber band around the canister so that it is 1 cm from the bottom end.

(2) Predict the quantity of pennies it takes to sink the canister to the 1 cm mark. Think carefully about your predictions—is there a pattern?

(3) Test and record in Data Collection Table #1 for each of the different cm marks.

(4) Record the whole-class data in Data Collection Table #2.

(5) Graph the data from Data Collection Table #2, with "Number of Pennies" on the vertical axis and "Depth of Canister" on the horizontal axis.

(6) Put a circle around all points. Draw a straight line, called the "Best Fit Line," through or between the pattern of points, showing the average class data.

Figure 5.2. Graph Title for Part 1: _____

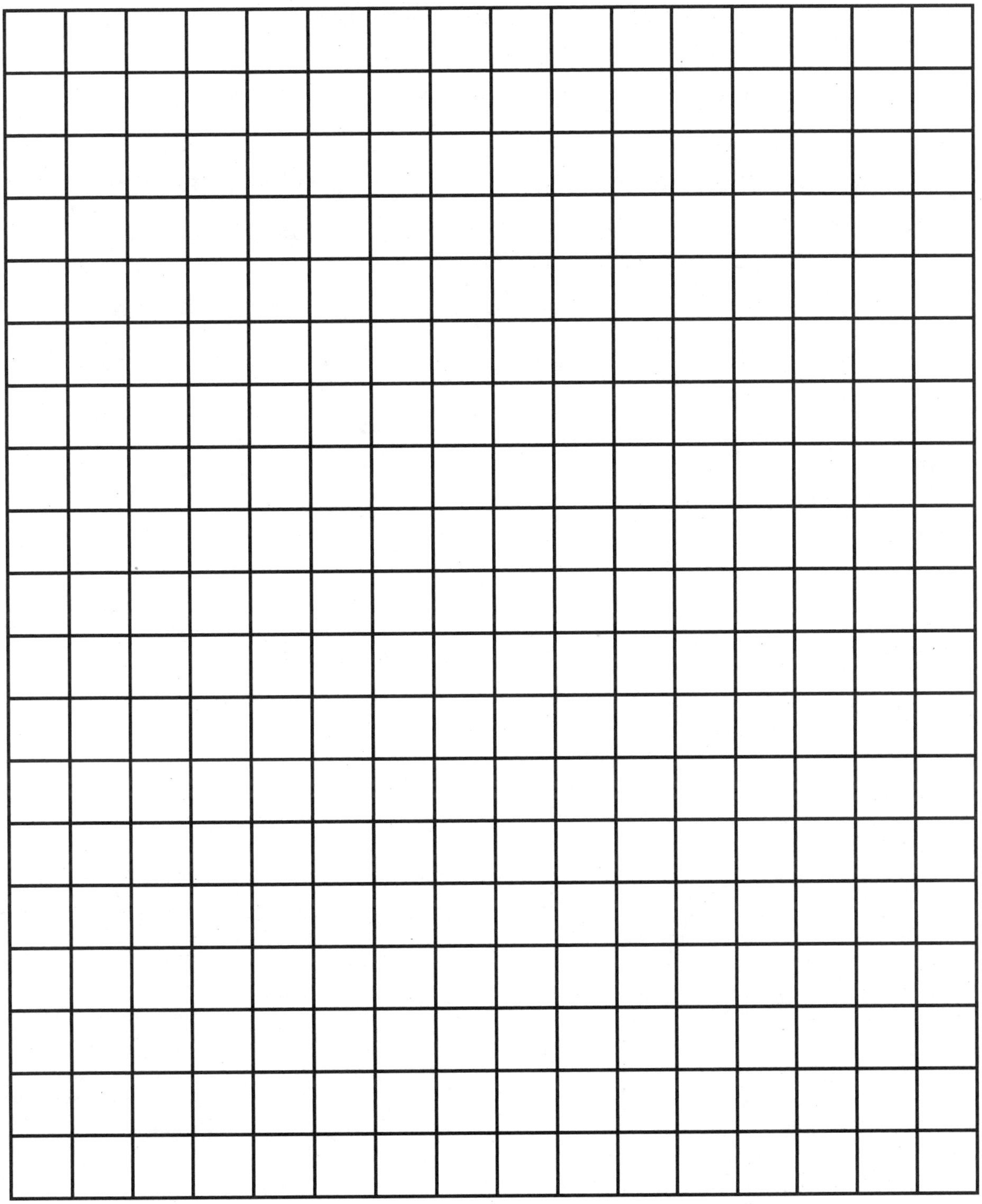

Procedures for Part 2:

(1) Use the Best Fit Line on your graph from Part 1 of Lab O-4 to find the average number of pennies for each depth. Record your observations in Data Collection Table #3.

(2) Predict the associated masses and record.

(3) Place the required amount of pennies for 1 cm in the canister. Measure the total mass of the canister and pennies. Record your observations.

(4) Test and adjust the mass with pennies to get the exact mass needed to sink the canister. Repeat for other lengths.

(5) Add your data to the whole-class data, in Data Collection Table #4.

(6) Make a graph of Data Collection Table #4, with the "Total Mass" on the vertical axis and "Length of Cylinder" on the horizontal axis. Draw a Best Fit Line to show the average line of data.

Figure 5.3. Graph Title for Part 2:

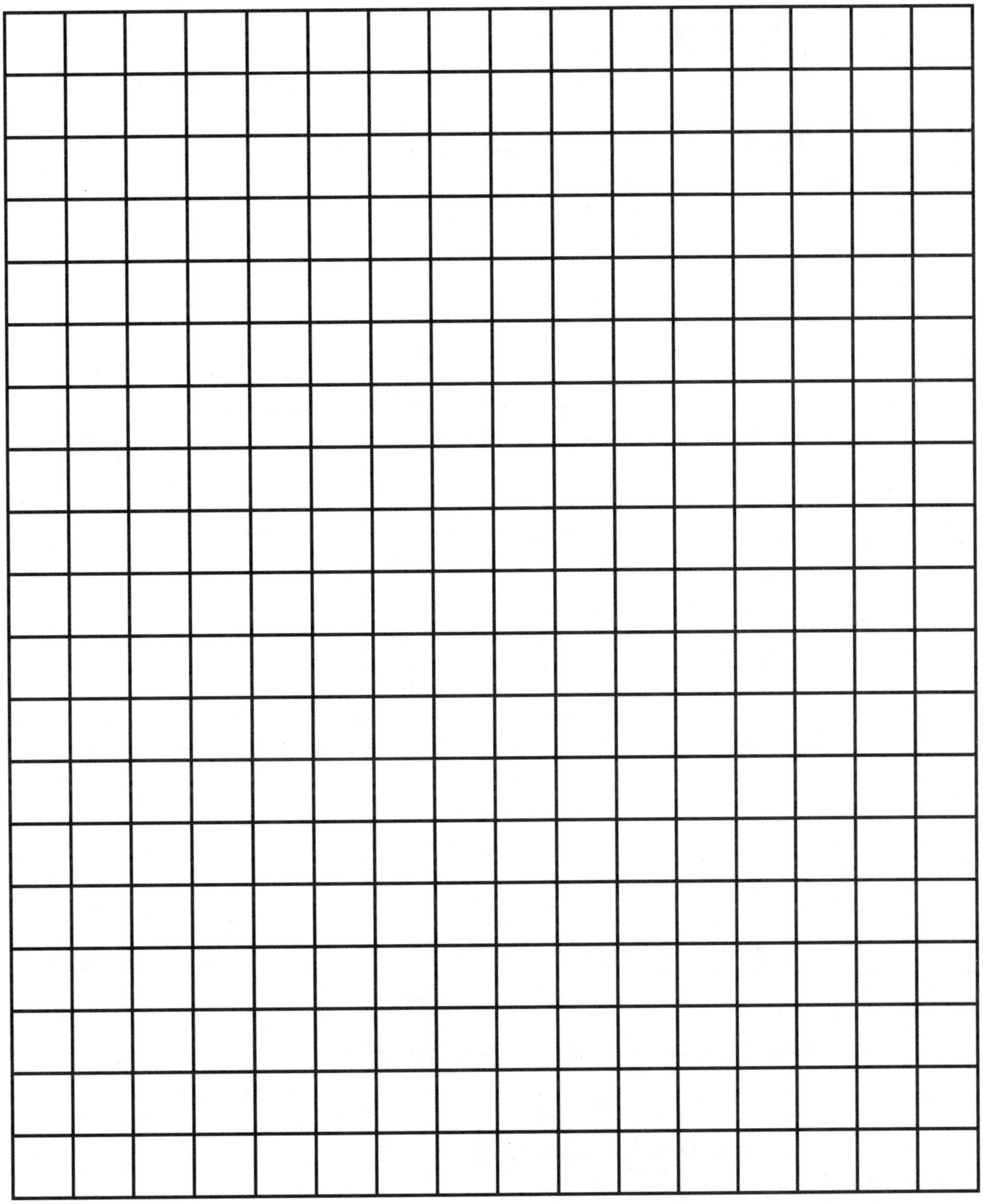

Lab Oceanography 5: (O-5) Barging Down the River

Part 1: (Teacher's Lesson Plan Outline)

Note: See Lesson Planning on page 32.

Anticipation Section Title: (O-5) Barging Down the River

Barges Inquiry Activity: The "barges" in this activity are rectangular plastic storage containers, without their lids. You can find many brands (Ziploc, etc.) of these water-proof containers in grocery stores, with metric measurements that range from 591 mL to 950mL. Students use any materials that would typically be set out for Lab O-5, to learn as much as they can about the influence that base area has on the depth of sinking. Give students 15 minutes in their lab groups with the materials, and then have the students report any findings to the class. When students are finished with these oral reports, continue on with Lab O-5.

Problem: If the same amount of water is put into barges of different sizes, how can you predict the depth to which each barge will sink into the water?

Prediction: Describe, in one sentence, your answer to the problem statement.

Thinking About the Problem: (See p. 235.)

Data Collection Materials and Procedures: (See p. 236.)

Safety Requirements: goggles, aprons

Expansion and Further Investigation:

(1) Describe exactly what you would need to know to predict how deep any ocean vessel would sink in water after it is loaded.

(2) Calculate the density of each of your "barges" from Lab O-5.

Part 2: (Student Lab Notebook Entries)

Anticipation Section Title: (O-5) Barging Down the River

Barges Inquiry Activity: Using the "barges" sitting at your lab table, try to determine what influence base area has on depth of sinking. You will have 15 minutes to learn all you can about this topic (base area vs. depth of sinking). As a lab group, you will report your findings to the rest of the class. When you are finished, we will complete the rest of our investigations.

Problem: If the same amount of water is put into barges of different sizes, how can you predict the depth to which each boat will sink into the water?

Prediction:

Note: Distribute the student handout (see *Part 3*) after students have completed their predictions.

Thinking About the Problem: Paraphrase the three main points of the reading in your own words.

(1)

(2)

(3)

Table 5.13. Data Collection Table #1: Data on Sinking Barges

Amount of Water (Ballast)	Size of Barge	Predicted Sinking Depth (cm)	Actual Sinking Depth (cm)
50 g	Small		
50 g	Large		
100 g	Small		
100 g	Large		
150 g	Small		
150 g	Large		

Table 5.14. Data Collection Table #2: Data on Barge Base Area

Barge	Length (cm)	Width (cm)	Base Area (cm²)
Small			
Large			

Table 5.15. Data Collection Table #3: Data on Submerged Volume of Barge With 100 g of Ballast

Barge	Ballast	Average Sinking Depth (cm)	Base Area (cm²)	Submerged Volume of Barge (cm³)
Small	100 g			
Large	100 g			

Analysis:

(1) How are the two barges similar? How do they differ from each other?

(2) How does the size of the barge relate to its depth of sinking in water?

(3) What is the submerged volume of each barge?

(4) Describe the overall relationship between the submerged volume and the depth of sinking in water for any barge.

Concluding-the-Analysis Statements:

(1) I learned...

(2) If I were to re-do this lab, I would change...

(3) An example of a variable in this lab is...

(4) An example of a control in this lab is...

Part 3: (Student Handout)

Note: Distribute to students after they complete the Prediction in *Part 2*.

Anticipation Section Title: (O-5) Barging Down the River

Thinking About the Problem

What is a barge? It is a large, flat-bottomed boat used primarily for the transportation of goods down a river. What is the purpose of ballast? *Ballast* is a nautical (*nauta*, "sailor" in Latin) term for mass carried by any floating ship. Any material added to a floating object to make it sit lower in the water is called ballast. Since ancient times, sailors have added ballast to their ships to make them more seaworthy. When the amount of ballast is kept constant, careful observers can begin to notice other characteristics of floating objects that influence how low they sit in water.

Knowing how high or low your boat will sit in water is vital for some occupations. Imagine the need for this knowledge as you journey down a long river on a barge, passing under bridges without hitting them. Imagine the need for navigating a large ocean vessel into a harbor, without hitting bottom. It is important to know the effect of ballast while floating any boat.

In the sinking canister experiment (Lab O-4) that you just completed, both the canister and the pennies had mass. You learned that the greater the mass of an object, the deeper it sinks. From the barges inquiry activity, you now know that the size of a barge (base area) can also play a role in how deep the barge sinks. In this lab you will investigate another property (volume) that might help us determine the depth of sinking.

Data Collection Materials:

- Bucket

- 600 mL barge

- 900 mL barge

- Metric ruler

- Rubber bands

- Water

Data Collection Procedures:

(1) Fill the smaller barge with 50 g of water. The water is ballast (50 mL of water has a mass of 50 g).

(2) Predict and record how deep the barge will sink in a bucket of water.

(3) Put the barge into a bucket of water. Move the rubber band to mark the depth to which the barge sinks when it is held level.

(4) Measure and record the actual depth of sinking, from the bottom of the barge to the rubber band.

(5) Put 50 g of water into the larger barge. Predict, how deep the larger barge will sink, then measure, and record how deep the larger barge actually sank.

(6) Fill the smaller barge 100 g of water and perform the same procedure as #2–#5. Then use 150 g of water.

(7) Measure and record the length and width of each barge. Calculate and record the base area of each barge.

(8) Transfer the appropriate data for the 100 g ballast barges into Data Collection Table #3. Calculate and record the submerged volume (the amount of space taken up by the barge underwater) of each barge.

SCI LINKS.
THE WORLD'S A CLICK AWAY

Topic: Mass

Go to: *www.scilinks.org*

Code: ESS037

SCI LINKS.
THE WORLD'S A CLICK AWAY

Topic: Mass and Volume

Go to: *www.scilinks.org*

Code: ESS038

Lab Oceanography 6: (O-6) Toying With Buoyancy

Part 1: (Teacher's Lesson Plan Outline)

Note: See Lesson Planning on page 32.

Anticipation Section Title: (O-6) Toying With Buoyancy

Problem: Can the volume of displaced water be predicted if the mass of a floating or sinking toy is known?

Prediction: Describe, in one sentence, how you could get a toy to sink or float just by changing its mass.

Thinking About the Problem: (See p. 241.)

Data Collection Materials and Procedures: (See p. 242.)

Safety Requirements: goggles, aprons

Expansion and Further Investigation:

(1) Determine, through experimentation, the densities of three different types of wood (e.g., oak or pine). Explain how these density results affect the floating level of the wood.

(2) Test any six toys (three that float, three that sink) in three new liquids. Record their performance, and comment on how the densities of the new liquids affect your results.

Part 2: (Student Lab Notebook Entries)

Anticipation Section Title: (O-6) Toying With Buoyancy

Problem: Can the volume of displaced water be predicted if the mass of a floating or sinking toy is known?

Prediction:

Note: Distribute the student handout (see *Part 3*) after students have completed their predictions.

Thinking About the Problem: Paraphrase the three main points of the reading in your own words.

(1)

(2)

(3)

Table 5.16. Data Collection Table #1: Data on the Volume of Water
Displaced by Toys

Buoyancy	Mass of Toy (g)	Predicted Water Displaced (mL)	Actual Water Displaced (mL)
Floating			
Floating			
Floating			
Sinking			
Sinking			
Sinking			

Table 5.17. Data Collection Table #2: Whole-Class Data on Floating
and Sinking Toys

Mass of Floating Toy (g)	Water Displaced by Floating Toy (mL)	Mass of Sinking Toy (g)	Water Displaced by Sinking Toy (mL)

Analysis:

(1) Using the class data and graph, what is the relationship between the mass of a floating toy and the volume of water it displaces?

(2) What is the relationship between the mass of a sinking toy and the volume of water it displaces?

(3) Imagine that you have a floating toy and a sinking toy of the same mass. Will they both displace the same amount of water? Explain your answer.

Concluding-the-Analysis Statements:

(1) I learned…

(2) If I were to re-do this lab, I would change…

(3) An example of a variable in this lab is…

(4) An example of a control in this lab is…

Part 3: (Student Handout)

Note: Distribute to students after they complete the Prediction in *Part 2.*

Anticipation Section Title: (O-6) Toying With Buoyancy

Thinking About the Problem

What makes a tub toy sink or stay afloat? In Labs O-4 and O-5, we investigated the buoyancy of canisters and boats. We know that there is a difference in buoyancy between an object that floats and an object that sinks. But a hypothesis that explains only a few situations would not be very useful. In science, we try to find a universal explanation—that is, an explanation that is useful in all related situations. In Lab 0-6, we are searching for a universal explanation of buoyancy.

We know that buoyancy depends on two main things: the mass of the object and the volume of water it displaces. Now we need to determine exactly what the relationship is between mass and volume of displaced water. This will allow us to explain the buoyancy of any object.

Data Collection Materials:

- Floating toys

- Graduated cylinder

- Large plastic bucket

- Sinking toys

- Triple beam balance

- Water

Data Collection Procedures:

(1) Use the triple beam balance to determine the mass of six toys, three that float and three that sink. Record the results.

(2) Predict the volume of water that will be displaced by each toy. Record the results.

(3) Measure and record the actual volume of water displaced by each toy.

(4) Select two toys, one floating and one sinking, about which you feel most confident in terms of data collection. Re-measure them, finding an average, and record the results on the whole-class data table.

(5) Graph the whole class data, with mass on the horizontal axis and volume of displaced water on the vertical axis.

(6) Color the large dots for floating toys a different color from the large dots for sinking toys.

Figure 5.4. Graph Title for Procedure #5: _____

Lab Oceanography 7: (O-7) Toying With Density

Part 1: (Teacher's Lesson Plan Outline)

Note: See Lesson Planning on page 32. We suggest that you review the concept of density prior to doing Lab O-7. Have students draw a Density Concept Flow Map (see Appendix B, p. 283) in their notebooks, reminding them of the various methods used to determine an object's density.

Anticipation Section Title: (O-7) Toying With Density

Problem: How are the densities of toys that float different from toys that sink?

Prediction: Describe, in one sentence, how density is related to floating and sinking.

Thinking About the Problem: (See p. 248.)

Data Collection Materials and Procedures: (See p. 249.)

Note: Overflow containers can be relatively easily constructed, if purchasing the items is not an option. Use large plastic drinking cups from fast-food restaurants. Cut 5 cm pieces of drinking straws. Hot glue them to a hole in the top edge of the plastic cup.

Safety Requirements: goggles, aprons

SCI**LINKS.**
THE WORLD'S A CLICK AWAY

Topic: Density of Water
Go to: *www.scilinks.org*
Code: ESS039

National Science Teachers Association

Expansion and Further Investigation:

(1) If a toy is to be put into a container of a liquid other than water, can you predict whether it will float at the surface, subsurface float, or sink to the bottom? How do the different liquids affect the situation?

(2) Graph the data of the mass and volume of all of the objects. Draw a straight line from the origin to each plotted point. You may extend the line beyond the point. Determine what the mass of one cm^3 of each object would be, then use that on the graph to determine the density of each object. Show your work.

Part 2: (Student Lab Notebook Entries)

Anticipation Section Title: (O-7) Toying With Density

Problem: What are the densities of toys that float? Of toys that sink?

Prediction:

Note: Distribute the student handout (see *Part 3*) after students have completed their predictions.

Thinking About the Problem: Paraphrase the three main points of the reading in your own words.

   (1)

   (2)

   (3)

Table 5.18. Data Collection Table #1: Data on the Densities of Floating Toys

Toy Description	Mass of Toy (g)	Volume of Toy (mL)	Density of Toy (g/mL)

Table 5.19. Data Collection Table #2: Data on the Densities of Sinking Toys

Toy Description	Mass of Toy (g)	Volume of Toy (mL)	Density of Toy (g/mL)

Analysis:

(1) Describe, in detail, the relationship between density and whether a toy floats or sinks.

(2) Imagine you need to describe density to a second grader in very simple terms (no mathematical terms). Write what you would say to describe density.

(3) How do the densities of toys that sink compare to toys that float?

Concluding-the-Analysis Statements:

(1) I learned…

(2) If I were to re-do this lab, I would change…

(3) An example of a variable in this lab is…

(4) An example of a control in this lab is…

Part 3: (Student Handout)

Note: Distribute to students after they complete the Prediction in *Part 2*.

Anticipation Section Title: (O-7) Toying With Density

Thinking About the Problem

Do you know how to measure density? The density (*densus*, "thick" in Latin) of any object is equal to its mass divided by its volume (g/mL). It can be thought of as a ratio of how much mass something has for how much space it takes up. You can measure an object's volume in two ways. The first, which you learned in Lab G-1, is by calculating its length **x** width **x** height measurement to get its volume (cm³). The second is by measuring the amount of water it displaces when completely submerged to get volume (mL). One cm³ equals one mL, and both measure volume. To use a pun which may make you groan, do you know why water is wonderful? The answer: since *one* mL of water weighs *one* g, water has a density of *one* g/mL and is therefore especially "*one*"-derful.

The concept of density underlies the explanation for a variety of natural phenomena, such as planetary composition, plate tectonics, weather patterns, and mineral formation. In addition, the depth to which any object sinks is related to its density. For an object to float, its mass must be equal to, or less than, the volume of the water it displaces. If the mass of an object is greater than the volume of the water it displaces, it will sink. In this lab, we will collect and compare density data for ten toys, five that float and five that do not.

Data Collection Materials:

- Calculator
- Floating toys
- Graduated cylinder
- Overflow container
- Sinking toys
- Triple beam balance

Data Collection Procedures:

(1) Select five toys that float in water. List them in Data Collection Table #1.

(2) Select five toys that sink completely in water. List them on Data Collection Table #2.

(3) Determine the mass of each of the 10 toys and record it on the appropriate table. Accuracy counts.

(4) Determine the volume of all 10 toys and record it on the appropriate table. Accuracy counts.

(5) Calculate the density for each toy and record it on the appropriate table.

Lab Oceanography 8: (O-8) Diving Into the Depths

Part 1: (Teacher's Lesson Plan Outline)

Note: See Lesson Planning on page 32.

Anticipation Section Title: (O-8) Diving Into the Depths

Problem: How does a Depth Diver operate?

Note: It may be helpful to whet the students' appetite for the experiment by briefly showing them the operation of a simple Depth Diver, using an inverted glass test tube half full of water. Use this quick demo to explain surface floating, subsurface floating, and resting on the bottom. Do not linger in this demonstration, however, because students will gather too many observations, making the inquiry nature of this lab less ideal.

Prediction: Describe, in one sentence, what the characteristics are of a good Depth Diver.

Thinking About the Problem: (See p. 256.)

Data Collection Materials and Procedures: (See p. 257.)

Safety Requirements: goggles, aprons

Table 5.20. Teacher Notes for Data Collection Table #1

Position of Diver	Volume of displaced water is greater than the original mass of Depth Diver.	Volume of displaced water is equal to the original mass of Depth Diver.	Volume of displaced water is less than the original mass of Depth Diver.
Surface float			X
Subsurface float		X	
Resting on the bottom	X		

Expansion and Further Investigation:

(1) Change additional variables (e.g., decrease the mass, increase the volume, or change the size of your container) on your Depth Diver project, doing more than what is required and adding challenge to the experiments you do for Lab O-8.

(2) Do the Sink a Sub Project (see Appendix B p. 284), demonstrating your results to the class.

Figure 5.5. Depth Diver Project Assignment Sheet

Depth Diver Project:

Your task is to build an original Depth Diver of your own. Your Depth Diver Project must have a creatively designed theme, which is followed by all of the "ingredients" involved in building your chosen diver.

Rules:

Build your Depth Diver using materials that can be found around your home.

Adjust your Depth Diver so it is easy for you to control.

Present your Depth Diver to your classmates.

Draw a diagram of your Depth Diver. Your drawing should be neat and colorful, have all the parts labeled, and have a title that describes your chosen theme.

Write a description of your Depth Diver. Your description should be a one-paragraph, complete explanation of how and why your Depth Diver sinks and floats. This paragraph must include what physical changes are going on with the Depth Diver so that it can change position ("volume" and "mass"). If you're not sure how to do this, then reread the Thinking About the Problem section of Lab O-8.

If you are unable to make your Depth Diver operate properly, you can still get partial credit by bringing your Depth Diver(s) to class to show what you have attempted. Explain to the class the modifications that you made in your attempts to get your Diver(s) to work. Include a brief explanation of how your Depth Diver(s) should have worked.

SCI**L**INKS.
THE WORLD'S A CLICK AWAY

Topic: Fluids and Pressure

Go to: *www.scilinks.org*
Code: ESS040

<u>Figure 5.6. Depth Diver Student Design Template</u>

Descriptive Anticipation Section Title:

_____

Drawing of Depth Diver in Container:
(Drawing should be neat and colorful and have all parts labeled.)

Depth Diver Explanation:
Explain why the Depth Diver sinks and then re-floats. Include how the Depth Diver changes mass.

_____
_____
_____
_____
_____
_____
_____
_____
_____
_____

Part 2: (Student Lab Notebook Entries)

Anticipation Section Title: (O-8) Diving Into the Depths

Problem: How does a Depth Diver operate?

Prediction:

Note: Distribute the student handout (see *Part 3*) after students have completed their predictions.

Thinking About the Problem: Paraphrase the three main points of the reading in your own words.

(1)

(2)

(3)

Table 5.21. Data Collection Table #1: Data on Depth Diver

Position of Diver	The mass of the Depth Diver is greater than the displaced water.	The mass of the Depth Diver is equal to the displaced water.	The mass of the Depth Diver is less than the displaced water.
Surface float			
Subsurface float			
Resting on the bottom			

Analysis:

(1) Describe three characteristics of an ideal Depth Diver.

(2) Why does the Depth Diver float downward when you apply pressure to the container?

(3) Explain what causes the Depth Diver to rise in the water when you stop applying pressure to the container.

Concluding-the-Analysis Statements:

(1) I learned...

(2) If I were to re-do this lab, I would change...

(3) An example of a variable in this lab is...

(4) An example of a control in this lab is...

Part 3: (Student Handout)

Note: Distribute to students after they complete the Prediction in *Part 2*.

Anticipation Section Title: (O-8) Diving Into the Depths

Thinking About the Problem

Can you guess how a Depth Diver works? We have studied the effects of mass and size on the depth an object sinks. We have also measured the volume of water an object displaces. A Depth Diver is an object in which the amount of water can be regulated. The Depth Diver sinks when we squeeze the container because the displaced water has no place to go except into the Depth Diver and compress any air in it. This works because water has more mass than air. The more water inside the Depth Diver, the more mass it has, increasing its density and causing it to sink.

In this lab, we will investigate the conditions under which a Depth Diver floats at the surface, floats below the surface, and rests on the bottom of a container. We will look closely at the volume of water the Depth Diver displaces in these three positions, as well as how its mass changes during the investigation.

Data Collection Materials:

- Eyedropper

- Metal balls

- Model Depth Diver

- Paper clips

- Syringe

- Test tubes (glass and plastic)

- Water bottle with cap to serve as the container

Data Collection Procedures:

(1) Use the water bottle and eyedropper, experimenting to make your own Depth Diver.

(2) Exchange the eyedropper for a small glass test tube, experimenting to make the Depth Diver work.

(3) Exchange the glass test tube for a syringe, experimenting to make the Depth Diver work.

(4) Finally, exchange the syringe for a small plastic test tube, experimenting to make the Depth Diver work.

(5) Make an "X" under the accurate description in each column of Data Collection Table #1, to summarize your findings.

Appendix A: Materials List for Labs

- Alka-Seltzer tablets (two per lab group)

- Apron

- Basalt rock sample (one per lab station)

- Beaker tongs (one per lab group)

- Beakers, 150 mL

- Beakers, 250 mL

- Beakers, 600 mL

- Bunsen burner

- Butcher paper, 1m x 1m (one per lab group)

- Calcite mineral sample (one per lab station)

- Calculator

- Carbonated cola (one 2-liter bottle)

- Cardboard squares (classroom set of 3 in. x 3 in)

- Classroom weather station (if available)

- Clear drinking straws (two per student, used in two experiments)

- Clear plastic bin

- Coat hanger wire (for bending into tube-retrieval hooks)

- Colored pencils

- Conglomerate rock sample (one per lab station)

- Copper plate (one per lab station)

- Corks, #1

- Dish soap

- Drawing compasses (one per lab group)

- Dry ice (one pound for each of two experiments)

- Empty pop cans (4 per class)

- Eyedroppers (one per lab group and one per Lab S-1 solution)

- Feldspar mineral sample (one per lab station)

- Film canister (one per lab group)

- Floating toys that fit in overflow containers (obtain a wide variety by offering small prizes to students for bringing in donations of toys)

- Food coloring (small samples)

- Glass pitcher

- Glass plate, one per lab station

- Glass test tubes (0.5 dram)

- Glass test tubes, 35 dram or larger

- Glue

- Goggles

- Graduated cylinder, 250 mL (glass)

- Graduated cylinders, 100 mL (glass or plastic)

- Gypsum mineral sample (one per lab station)

- Halite mineral sample (one per lab station)

- Hammer

- Hand lenses (classroom set)

- Helium (one small canister)

- Hot plate

- Ice cubes (one bag)

- Index card (one package)

- Internet website access

- Iron nail, (one per lab station)

- Isopropyl (rubbing) alcohol, 50 mL

- Lamp

- Lamp oil, 100 mL

- Local newspapers

- Magnetite mineral sample (one per lab station)

- Marble rock sample (one per lab station)

- Masking tape

- Metal balls (steel shotgun shot works well)

- Methane (use Bunsen burner hookups)

- Metric rulers (classroom set)

- Metric thermometers (one per lab group)

- Milk carton containers, half gallon, cut down to three inches high (one per lab group)

- Milk carton containers, half pint, cut down to three inches high (one per lab group)

- Model Sun (large inflatable yellow ball)

- Notebook paper

- Obsidian rock sample (one per lab station)

- Overflow containers, can be homemade with large plastic drinking glasses, small straws, and hot glue (one per lab group)

- Paper clips

- Pennies (100)

- Plastic bags, 1 gallon (three)

- Plastic buckets, 1 gallon (one per lab group)

- Propane (one small canister)

- Protective gloves (one pair per lab group)

- Pumice rock sample (one per lab station)

- Pushpins of different colors

- Quartz mineral sample (one per lab station)

- Quartzite rock sample (one per lab station)

- Rectangular plastic storage containers, 600 mL and 900 mL (one pair per lab group)

- Rope or twine, 5 meters long (one per lab group)

- Rubber bands

- Sand (one bag)

- Sandstone rock sample (one per lab station)

- Saturated Epsom salt solution, 50 mL (650 g of Epsom salt in 1000 mL of water)

- Scissors (classroom set)

- Sewing thread (one spool)

- Shale rock sample (one per lab station)

- Shallow pan

- Sinking toys that fit in overflow containers (obtain a wide variety by offering small prizes to students for bringing in donations of toys)

- Slate rock sample (one per lab station)

- Sling psychrometers (one per partnership)

- Small aquarium

- Small blocks of clay (one per lab group)

- Small test tubes (assorted sizes, both glass and plastic)

- Soap-blown bubbles (one container)

- Soil (one bag)

- Syringes (small and no needles, one per lab group)

- Ten small landscape flags

- Test tubes (assortment of glass and plastic)

- Test tubes, 75 mm x 10 mm (three)

- Toothpick (one per student)

- Transparency sheet (one per lab group)

- Triple beam balances (one per lab group)

- Wall-size map of the world

- Water, 150 mL

- Water, 50 mL

- Water bottle with cap (empty) (one per lab group)

Appendix B: Additional Activities and Strategies

Figure 6.1. Predicting the Future

Directions for Predicting the Future:

Scientists make predictions based on what they observe about the world around them. A prediction (explaining a natural event) that a scientist makes is sometimes called an "educated guess." For example, "I predict it will be blue." (This is different from a hypothesis, which is an explanation that can be tested. For example, "It will be blue because blue is higher in energy.")

Use your surroundings and your knowledge about the world to make at least three predictions in each of the following categories. These predictions should be targeted to come true between now and the end of this school year.

Today's Date:
Your Family and Friends:
(1)
(2)
(3)
The United States:
(1)
(2)
(3)
The World:
(1)
(2)
(3)
Television and Movies:
(1)
(2)
(3)
Music and Theater:
(1)
(2)
(3)
Sports:
(1)
(2)
(3)
Our Middle School:
(1)
(2)
(3)
On the back of this page, trace your hand. Then, write the following sentence to complete your prediction: "I predict that my hand will (grow larger OR remain the same size) by the end of the school year."

Pretest for Earth Science Success

Directions: Because this is a pretest, it will not be scored for accuracy. This pretest covers 33 statements of general knowledge and concepts related to each lab in our Earth science curriculum. It serves as an advance organizer, helping you anticipate what you will be studying, and it allows the teacher to see where the largest gaps are in your understanding.

Read each sentence carefully. Determine whether you agree or disagree with the statement. Mark an "X" in the appropriate box. You will receive credit for effort.

Table 6.1. Pretest for *Earth Science Success*

#	Agree	Disagree	Statement
1			An inference is your interpretation or explanation of what you observe.
2			Very careful observers from many cultures were able to explain astronomical events mathematically, with reliability, predictability, and precision.
3			The sizes of the planets are immensely larger than the distance between the planets themselves.
4			Two of the most important process skills that scientists use every day are estimations of measurement and manipulation of standard laboratory equipment.
5			By comparing the Gas Giants and the Terrestrial planets we can gain insight into the formation of our weather.
6			The fraction of the light falling on a solar system object that is then reflected back into space is called its "lumen."
7			Differences between circumference of the Moon and Earth affect your survival, and changes would make your life very different.
8			An asteroid is a leftover remnant of the early formation of the solar system, with a magnificent tail that can stretch halfway across the sky.
9			The world's first artificial satellite, named Sputnik, was launched by the Soviet Union in 1957, and its job was to collect data on atmospheric temperatures.
10			Minerals are Earth materials that have four main characteristics: they are solid, inorganic, and naturally occurring, and they have a definite chemical structure.
11			Scientists use various properties—such as hardness, luster, color, and, specific gravity—to help identify rocks.
12			There are three main groups of rocks: igneous, sedimentary, and metamorphic.
13			Through research and evidence, including the use of the geologic time scale, most scientists conclude that the Earth is approximately 4.6 billion years old.

14			Within layers of atmosphere there are records of events that have occurred on Earth, including the remains and/or imprints of the different plants and animals that have lived on Earth.
15			Soil textures are determined by the percentages of clay, silt, and sand that are found in the soil.
16			An earthquake is the result of a sudden release of energy in the Earth's crust that creates seismic waves.
17			Volcanoes form where magma burns through the crust at subduction zones, at spreading centers, or at "hot spots" like Hawaii.
18			The continuous movement of water in a cyclic pattern is called the carbon cycle.
19			The instrument used to measure atmospheric pressure is called a thermometer and it is essential in weather forecasting.
20			A phase change refers to whether a substance like water is a solid (ice), liquid (water), or a gas (water vapor).
21			Relative humidity is a measure of how much water vapor is actually in the air compared with the amount the air could possibly hold.
22			When a warm air mass meets a cool air mass, two distinct bodies of air are brought in contact, each with its own temperature and relative humidity.
23			When the air is cool, it cannot hold as much water vapor as when the air is warm, and therefore, more water will evaporate.
24			By including information from a number of different stations, weather maps give a good idea of what the weather is across the whole area represented.
25			It is possible to predict long-term weather changes with some accuracy just by looking at the clouds.
26			Large amounts of air must be added to water to achieve even a relatively small change in temperature.
27			Although water is the most abundant substance on Earth's surface, very little of it is pure hydrogen and oxygen.
28			Since water is more easily moved than land, ocean water gets pulled over the land area that happens to be facing the Moon, causing the side of the Earth closest to the Moon to experience higher tides.
29			Buoyancy is actually a result of the water pushing upward on objects.
30			When the amount of ballast is kept constant, careful observers can begin to notice other characteristics of floating objects that influence how low they sit in water.
31			We know that buoyancy depends on two main things: the mass of the object and the area of water it displaces.
32			For an object to float, its mass must be equal to or greater than the volume of the water it displaces.
33			A Depth Diver sinks when we squeeze the bottle because the displaced water has no place to go except into the Depth Diver. The water then removes any air in the Depth Diver.

Teacher Notes on Pretest for *Earth Science Success*: Answers that should have been marked "disagree," along with a brief explanation, include: #3 (smaller, not larger), #5 (solar system, not weather), #6 (albedo, not lumen), #7 (environments, not circumference), #8 (comet, not asteroid), #11 (minerals, not rocks), #14 (rocks, not atmosphere), #18 (hydrologic, not carbon), #19 (barometer, not thermometer), #23 (less, not more), #25 (short-term, not long-term), #26 (energy, not air), #31 (volume, not area), #32 (less, not greater), and #33 (compress, not remove).

Earth Science Bingo

Walk around the room and introduce yourself to your classmates. If your classmate can agree with one of these Earth-science-related statements in a bingo square below, write his/her name in the square. Fill in the whole bingo board (not just a row or column) then sit back down in your seat. Each student's name can appear only once on your bingo board. You can use your own name in only one square.

I went for a full day hike in nature this summer.	This summer, I visited a state that has had an earthquake.	I like to look at the stars and planets in the night sky.	I know a scientific term in Latin or Greek.	Autumn is my favorite season.
I like to do experiments and write up detailed lab reports!	I like to sketch and draw what I see.	I read a science-related book this summer.	I have seen a volcano.	I have liked dinosaurs since I was a little kid.
I would like to become an astronaut and go visit Mars.	I like to wonder about things that go on in the world around me.	**Free Space**	I play a musical instrument that uses wind to make sound.	My favorite TV show is the weather portion of the evening news.
I have seen a double rainbow.	I have collected rocks.	I visited a rock formation, geyser, or hot springs this summer.	I can name the Earth's closest star.	I visited a state or national park this summer.
I have witnessed the launch of a space shuttle.	I think science is really great!	I can explain why we have seasons on Earth.	I can explain why we see different phases of the Moon.	I can name a famous scientist.

Panel of Five

There are several ways in which a teacher can use an article from a publication to enhance classroom instruction. One of those ways is a game called Panel of Five, which has proved to be very successful as an instructional tool with early adolescents. Use "The Legend of Orion the Hunter" (p. 271) for this first game, so students can develop good game skills while studying astronomy-related topics. As with all instructional strategies, variety is the best policy. The rules of the game are shown below:

A. Panel of Five is a fun method used to teach students about the content from any science-related newspaper, magazine, or legend. The teacher needs to make about 35 photocopies of the article and buy six inexpensive prizes per class. (We suggest cheap prizes from the birthday aisle at local discount stores.)

B. Panel of Five begins by selecting (randomly) one student to be "director" and five students to start out as "panel members." The rest of the students sit in a half-circle facing the five panel members. Illustration 6.1 shows the classroom arrangement.

Illustration 6.1. Panel of Five

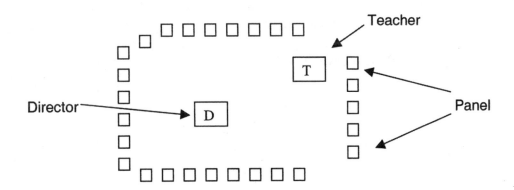

C. There are three rules in Panel of Five. First, no fill-in-the-blank style questions can be asked. Students must instead ask good, challenging questions that start with a *what, where, when, why,* or *how* or are true/false. Second, once a panel member has answered a question correctly, she/he does not need to answer another question until the next paragraph is read. Third, one spelling question is allowed per paragraph. This sometimes helps challenge hard-to-eliminate students from the panel, especially when they don't get to see the words.

D. The panel members do not get to have an article in front of them (they have to use listening skills only). The teacher's job (along with classroom management) is to read clearly, paragraph by paragraph, whenever the director tells you. The student director runs the classroom, calling on four or five students per paragraph (turn by turn). The student, when called upon, would ask a particular panel member a question about the paragraph that was just read. If the panel member answers it correctly, then she/he gets to stay on the panel. If the panel member answers it incorrectly, then the student who asked the question gets to be on the panel. The director says "switch" or "stay" after the panel member has given his/her response, and then the director calls on the next student to ask a question.

E. At the end of class, the five panel members who are on the panel each get a prize, and so does the director. This makes a total of six prizes distributed per class.

F. Students can cover about 8–10 paragraphs in an average 50-minute class period. If the article or story has very short paragraphs, several paragraphs could be covered at a time. "The Legend of Orion the Hunter" (see p. 271) could be used to initiate discussions on stars in the sky. Science-related current events, from newspapers, journals, and online sources, can easily be used in Panel of Five, as well.

The Legend of Orion the Hunter

Paul was a brave, young boy who lived with his grandfather in the village of Dakota. Paul helped his grandfather around the house, worked in the garden, and took care of the animals on their farm. There was not much time for Paul to play. Each week, Paul walked with his grandfather to Lake Batavia to get water.

One day, his grandfather became very ill. "Paul, you must go for water by yourself," his grandfather told him. "But you must only go to Lake Batavia. Do not go to the Cedar River," he warned.

"But, Grandfather," Paul pleaded, "the water in the Cedar River is very fresh and clear. It twinkles like the stars at night. And it is much closer than Lake Batavia. I can be back with water very fast, if I go to the river."

"That is true, my grandson," he said. "But the water in the Cedar River belongs to Orion, the fierce hunter of the Dakota region. Orion will kill you if you go near his river."

Paul started down the road to Lake Batavia. He had worked very hard that week and quickly became tired. "I can't possibly walk all the way to Lake Batavia," he thought. "I will take only a little water from the Cedar River. The hunter will never know." So Paul walked across the field to the river.

Just as Paul dipped his bucket into the water, Orion the Hunter burst forth from the water, with a brilliant fire on the tip of his sword and sparkling gems lining his belt. "What are you doing near my river?" the hunter bellowed fiercely.

Paul was so startled that he almost dropped his bucket in the river. "I am only getting a very small amount of water for my grandfather," he pleaded. "He is very sick, and I am so tired from working all week. I cannot walk all the way to Lake Batavia. Please, you have so much water here in this river. I only need a little."

The hunter paused for a moment. "Well, all right," he mumbled. "Just this once: Fill your buckets and leave immediately."

"Thank you, Orion, sir," Paul said. Paul began filling his bucket with the pure river water. When he had filled his buckets, Paul thanked Orion and left.

The next week, Paul again was going for water. "I should tell Mr. Orion that my grandfather is feeling better," he thought. So he headed down to the river.

As Paul approached the Cedar River, Orion burst forth, shooting a brilliant fire off the tip of his sword. "What are you doing near my river?" the hunter bellowed.

"It is Paul," he answered quickly. "I came to tell you that my grandfather drank your water and now he is finally feeling better. May I please have a little more water from your river?"

Orion felt sorry for Paul. He muttered, "Well, all right, just this once: Fill your buckets and leave."

The next week Paul met a kind-hearted young girl, named Lara, with two small water buckets. "Are you going for water with those tiny buckets?" he asked.

"My mother is sick, and these buckets are as large as I can carry," Lara said.

Paul led Lara down to the Cedar River. As they approached, Orion's brilliant belt forewarned of the fire-tipped sword that would soon threaten them. "What are you doing near my river?"

"It is Paul with a girl, named Lara, and she has two very small water buckets. She needs your water to save her mother, who is very sick," he said.

"Those are small buckets," Orion said. He lowered his shining sword and mumbled, "Well, all right, just this once: Fill your buckets and leave."

Both Paul and Lara thanked Orion for their water.

Week after week, Paul and Lara went to the Cedar River to fill their buckets. Each time, Orion would burst forth with his brilliant belt and flaming sword and ask, "What are you doing near my river?" Then he would hear their story and say, "Well, all right, just this once: Fill your buckets and leave."

One week, when Paul and Lara were going to the river, they met a strong young man, named Daniel. The young man was carrying three buckets.

"Are you going for water?" Paul asked.

"Yes," said Daniel. "But I am afraid I will not be able to walk much farther. I am carrying these three buckets in order to help others out."

"It is not far," replied Paul, "just to the river."

"You cannot get water from the river. Orion will hit you with his flaming sword. You must get water only from Lake Batavia," commented Daniel.

"That is silly," said Paul. "Orion the Hunter is my friend. He will not hurt a generous young man like you. Come with us."

Paul did not want Orion to burst forth and scare Daniel, so he ran ahead. "Orion," he called. "I have brought a generous young man carrying three buckets, to help others out. He cannot make it to the lake. Please, let him have some river water.

And, please do not threaten him with your fiery sword because that might push him away."

Slowly, Orion came out of the water. He lowered his shining sword and said, "Well, all right, just this once: Fill his buckets and leave."

The generous young man thought Paul was exceedingly clever and told the village about taking water from the Cedar River. Soon many people came to the river and filled their buckets. Orion never bothered them.

When Orion continued to not harm or threaten them, the people began to tell stories that the fierce hunter must have been killed. Orion seemed to no longer guard the Cedar River.

Paul could not believe these stories. He ran to the river, "Orion, Orion," he shouted. But Orion did not appear. Paul ran up and down the river, searching for Orion. Finally, Paul collapsed, yelling, "I did not mean to hurt you, Orion. You are my friend. Please come and talk to me," he pleaded.

Very slowly, Orion and his brilliant belt appeared above the water. "Please do not be frustrated," he said to Paul. "I am at fault. I was given this Cedar River water by the gods of sea and sky to protect. I have failed to protect it. I will never get to protect any water again."

"But you are so kind and good," replied Paul. "I will go to the temple tonight and talk to the gods of sea and sky. There must be other water for you to protect."

That night Paul, Lara, and Daniel went to the temple. "Please, give Orion new water. We don't want him to die," they begged. "He is good and has helped many of us," they said. They told the gods of sea and sky the many stories of Orion's kindness. The gods were very impressed by Orion.

As the three walked home in the dark, suddenly a bright flash was seen in the sky. They all looked up. There, high above them was the tip of Orion's brilliant shining sword, proudly held to protect all of the waters of the seas and the stars of the sky. Orion the Hunter was positioned directly across from a big water dipper constellation to remind people of his kindness. Paul, Lara, and Daniel knew that Orion the Hunter was finally happy.

Tic-Tac-Know

This choice-oriented listing of assignments is related to the Sun, Earth, and Moon system. It is designed to encourage collecting and categorizing of data, as well as application, analysis, and extensions of your learning. It uses two educational strategies, called Gardner's Multiple Intelligences and Bloom's Taxonomy, to challenge you as an individual while you learn.

You must select and skillfully complete one activity from each horizontal row on the Tic-Tac-Know Options Board. This will help you, and potentially others, learn more about the Sun, Earth, and Moon system. Remember to make your work rich in detail, thoughtful, original, and accurate.

Table 6.2. Tic-Tac-Know Options Board

	Logical-Mathematical	**Spatial-Artistic**	**Bodily-Kinesthetic**
Knowledge and Comprehension	Make a timeline showing the history of human space flight, for all countries, from 1957 to the present.	Draw a colored and labeled diagram, on a poster, showing how the composition of Earth's atmosphere changes with altitude.	Plan for and involve the entire class in an exercise-related activity that teaches us about the many phases of the Moon.
Application	Show the relationships between an actual tide chart for a West coast city beach and the phases of the Moon.	Design a wall mural that can be used to show the changes in the Sun-Earth system that cause each different season.	Make a model that shows how global warming can be affected by greenhouse gases.
Analysis and Synthesis	Develop and present a PowerPoint presentation that dispels five common misconceptions that students have about the Sun, Earth, and Moon system.	Create an information-filled comic book that lists at least 10 things that an average middle school student could do to live a carbon-neutral life.	Prepare and present a skit to the class that shows details about how life would be different if we lived on another planet.

Edible Stalactites and Stalagmites

Problem: Have you ever imagined eating stalactites or stalagmites? Stalactites grow from the ceilings of caves, gradually getting longer as calcium carbonate ($CaCO_3$) deposits drip down and crystallize. Stalagmites pile up on the floor of caves, beneath the stalactites. You can grow crystals just like them in your own kitchen. Rock candy (large sugar crystals) grows in a similar way to stalactites and stalagmites.

Prediction: How long do you predict it will take to grow an edible crystal?

Data Collection Materials:

- 250 mL (1 cup) of water

- 500 mL (2 cups) of granulated sugar

- Coffee filter strip (or cotton string)

- Large drinking glass or other glass jar

- Paper clip

- Pencil

- Small saucepan

Data Collection Procedures:

(1) Clean all materials (saucepan, glass, paper clip) thoroughly—otherwise the crystals will not form.

(2) Bring the water to a boil in the saucepan.

(3) As soon as the water boils, turn off the heat and begin stirring in the sugar.

(4) Continue adding the sugar until no more will dissolve.

(5) Allow the solution to cool for about 10 minutes.

(6) Pour the solution into the drinking glass.

(7) Rub some sugar onto the string so the crystals will stick to it.

(8) Tie one end of the string to the pencil, and then rest the pencil on the rim of the glass.

(9) Put the glass in a place where it will remain relatively cool and completely undisturbed for several days.

Illustration 6.2. Stalactite and Stalagmite

Vocabulary of Geology Notes

After learning the definition, draw a sketch that will help you remember both the word and its meaning.

1.

Atom:
Smallest particle of matter that still has all of the properties (e.g., color and odor) of that matter. If broken down any further, it loses those properties.

2.

Molecule:
A group of two or more atoms that are chemically bonded together (e.g., water molecules are made of hydrogen and oxygen).

3.

Table of Elements:
List of all the atoms that are fundamental building blocks for all things on Earth and in space. Elements make up minerals.

4.

Minerals:
Naturally occurring elements, that exist in a crystal form (patterns). Minerals make up rocks and gemstones.

5.

Rocks:
Natural mixture of minerals. They can be formed into one of three types: igneous, metamorphic, and sedimentary.

Periodic Puns

Knowledge of the periodic table of elements helps geologists identify minerals in rocks. With some imagination and a pun now and then, it is possible to use the names of elements as synonyms or substitutes for some phrases. So "cesium" your pen and fill in the blanks. But be careful, because spelling counts!

Element Name:	Atomic Number:	Phrase:
1.	#	What a good doctor does for her patients
2.	#	Police officer
3.	#	Have went (very poor grammar)
4.	#	Funeral chant (very rude)
5.	#	Holmium x 0.5 =
6.	#	Chemical Apache (politically incorrect)
7.	#	To press a shirt
8.	#	To guide (past tense)
9.	#	A kitchen work area with a drain
10.	#	An amusing prisoner
11.	#	The Lone Ranger's horse
12.	#	Mickey Mouse's dog
13.	#	It's found on a sul
14.	#	View by a person named Cal
15.	#	Two equal a dime
16.	#	Funds from your mother's sister
17.	#	What carpenters do before the roofing
18.	#	Superman's greatest enemy
19.	#	Name of a Nobel Prize winner
20.	#	The planet closest to the Sun
21.	#	You knelt down to put your ___ it
22.	#	The thing that grinds garbage

Periodic Puns Answers:

1. Helium #2 and Curium #96

2. Copper #29

3. Argon #18

4. Barium #56

5. Hafnium #72

6. Indium #49

7. Iron #26

8. Lead #82

9. Zinc #30

10. Silicon #14

11. Silver #47

12. Plutonium #94

13. Sulfur #16

14. Calcium #20

15. Nickel #28

16. Antimony #51

17. Fluorine #9

18. Krypton #36

19. Einsteinium #99

20. Mercury #80

21. Neon #10

22. Disprosium #66

Weather Instrument Project

Students will construct a weather instrument, conduct research on the instrument, and use the instrument that they built to record measurements of current weather conditions for seven days. This is an at-home project. It is to be done individually, not with partners.

Students will begin by selecting one of the following weather instruments. Two of the instruments provide less challenge, and therefore result in a slightly lower grade. The choices are as follows:

(1) Anemometer

(2) Barometer

(3) Hygrometer

(4) Precipitation Gauge (The highest grade possible is B, 85%.)

(5) Thermometer

(6) Wind Vane (The highest grade possible is B, 85%.)

Students may use internet sites or library resources to research the following information:

(1) What the weather instrument is used for; its purpose;

(2) How the weather instrument works; its mechanics;

(3) How to build their own version of the weather instrument; and

(4) The story of a scientist who either invented, or is known for using, the weather instrument.

After constructing the instrument, the students will use it to record the measurements of current weather conditions. Students must take measurements at least three different times per day for seven consecutive days. Data must be collected that can be recorded on both a data table and a graph. This data should include verification for accuracy by checking/comparing with actual weather instrument data (use internet sites, television and radio broadcasts, classroom weather stations, and newspapers).

The project will be presented to classmates on _____. The instrument and a poster showing research results, at least one data table and at least one graph, should be referred to during the presentation.

Table 6.3. A Sample Data Table (to help get you started).

Date	Time of Day	Weather Instrument Reading	Verified Actual Readings	Other Observations

Density Concept Flow Map

A concept flow map can be used by students to develop a better understanding of the various methods used to determine the density of an object. The three examples (rectangular objects, smaller nonrectangular objects, and larger nonrectangular objects) are represented in the picture below, which was modeled on a student's notebook entry.

Figure 6.2. Concept Map on Density

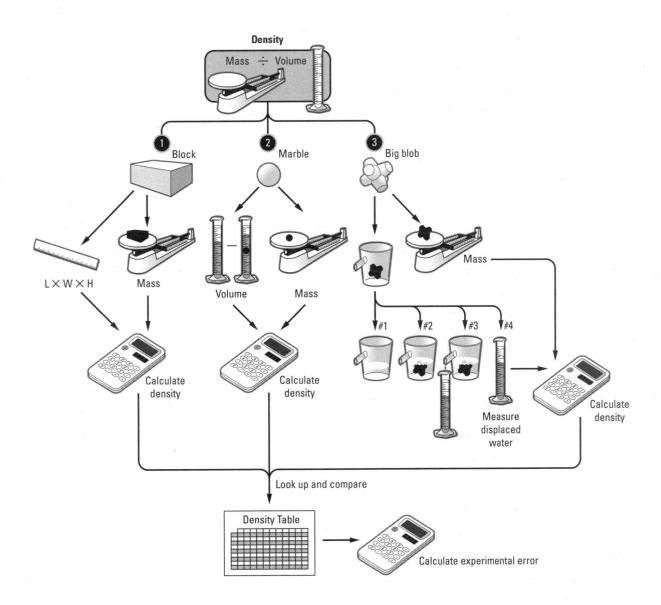

Sink a Sub Project

Problem: Design, construct, and demonstrate a device that will float for at least three seconds, sink to the bottom of our classroom aquarium, and then float again. The demonstration tank is 30 cm deep.

Requirements: You will design and construct a Sink a Sub device. You will do a presentation on this submarine-like device (presenting it to the class). You will also give a name to your Sink a Sub device that helps describe it in some way.

Restrictions: You will only have five minutes to get your sub to complete its mission. Presentations will be done using our class aquarium. You may not touch (or drop things onto) the sub once it is put into the water—it must be completely self-operational. Materials may not cling to the walls or be connected to anything outside the tank. Chemical reactions are not recommended. No chemicals may enter the tank water. All must be contained inside the sub and not released into the aquarium. The density of the water in the aquarium must remain unchanged after your sub runs its course. Things that dissolve, or come apart, in water (e.g., tissues and paper) are not allowed.

Sink a Sub Presentation:

(1) Describe all of the materials needed to construct your final design, as well as any materials that you tried but decided not to use.

(2) Explain how the Sink a Sub works in detail. How does it change density? (It should change density twice.) Describe what is causing the density to change. Use the words *mass* and *volume* in your description.

(3) Originality, creativity, and problem-solving skills are essential.

Helpful Notes:

(1) Ideas for getting started:

$$\text{Density} = \frac{\text{Mass}}{\text{Volume}}$$

(2) Ways to make a Sink a Sub sink:
Increase mass: slowly take on water
Decrease volume: give off a gas

(3) Ways to make a Sink a Sub float:
        Decrease mass: leave ballast behind
        Increase volume: generate a gas

Evaluation Criteria:

(1) Did the Sink a Sub make a complete round-trip?

(2) Did the Sink a Sub design show creativity, originality, complexity, effort, and dedication?

(3) Did you fully describe the design process to the class? Did you share the complete description of how you arrived at your final submarine design (including attempts, failures, successes, and frustrations)?

(4) Did you fully describe how the Sink a Sub operates (describing the two changes in density during your explanation)?

(5) Were you able to complete the round-trip in less than five minutes?

(6) Were you respectful of others during their presentations?

Science Experiment Project

Parent Explanation Cover Letter

Dear Science Students and Parents:

All science students are required to complete a Science Experiment Project. This Science Experiment Project will be due on _____. A Science Project Gallery Walk will be held on _____, during which the students will briefly show and tell others about their projects. In addition, some students (depending on which category they choose) will be offered the opportunity (optional) to enter their project into the district K–12 science fair, which takes place on _____.

Students must develop a controlled experiment in one of four science fields: Earth science, life science, physical science, or consumer science. This experiment must deal with a real-world issue (working toward the solution of a societal/community-ty-based dilemma). Its goal is the pursuit of a question about which the student is curious.

For the Experiment Project Categories: Earth sciences include environmental issues, astronomy, meteorology, geology, weathering/erosion, topography, physical oceanography, etc. Life sciences include anatomy, health/wellness, human behavior, plant growth, pesticide/fertilizer/herbicide applications, reaction times, etc. physical sciences include chemistry, forces, speed, acceleration, renewable energy sources, electricity, magnetism, etc. Consumer science topics include experimenting on different brands of a particular product to determine the best overall product. Although this category choice would not allow a student to participate in the district science fair (participation is not required), it may provide an interesting, real-life option for many.

Major portions of the project have been broken down into smaller steps, with various due dates. The "Due Dates for Science Experiment Project" handout will help the student monitor his/her progress. A detailed form describing how the "Science Experiment Presentation Poster" should look and a "Presentation Grading Rubric" are also provided. Finally, a form describing the requirements involved in generating three "Multiple-Choice Questions for the Audience" during each student's presentation is included as well.

Students will not be allowed to work in groups for this assignment. A simple poster, displaying results, is required. The students will be giving a presentation about their project to the class. You are invited to attend your son/daughter's presentation. The presentations will be held during science class, beginning the week of _____ (order will be determined on _____). All students must be prepared to present on ___. You are also invited to attend the Gallery Walk on _____(held during science class).

This entire project is made up of small assignments, culminating in a poster (with word-processed text) and a class presentation. This project can be thought of as a do-it-yourself, real-world, laboratory experiment. The critical part is that this is an experiment, not a demonstration and not a research paper. It is worth 100 points.

Good luck!

Table 6.4. Due Dates for Science Experiment Project

Required Task	Due Date	Point Value
Select a title and category (Consumer, Earth, Life, or Physical Science)		10
Problem statement phrased as a question)		10
Hypothesis		10
Background research	Do not hand in, just keep working on it throughout the project, using it to form your conclusions and guide your experiments. Any findings will be written in your "Thinking About the Problem" paragraphs.	
Materials list		10
Procedure steps (and labeled sketch)		10
Record all observations	Do not hand in, just keep working on it throughout the project, using it to form your conclusions and guide your experiments.	
Analyze data, draw conclusions	Do not hand in, just keep working on it throughout the project, using it to form your conclusions and guide your experiments.	
Prepare for presentation	Do not hand in, just keep working on it throughout the project, using it to form your conclusions and guide your experiments.	
Give presentation to class		50
Science Project Gallery Walk		Not Graded
Total points possible	100	

Science Experiment Presentation Poster: All portions must use correct grammar, punctuation, spelling, and mechanics. All text should be word-processed (sketches, graphs, and daily logs can be handwritten, however). Ask an adult to help by proof-reading the requirements on page 289–290.

Title and Category: The title of your experiment project should be several descriptive words, not a complete sentence, dealing with the chosen topic of your experiment. It should be brief but it should also indicate the variable(s) that will be tested. (An example of a poor title is: "The Best Table Napkin." A better title would be: "Investigation of the Absorbency, Durability, and Strength of Table Napkins.") The category should be one of the following sciences: Earth, life, physical, or consumer science.

Problem: Explicitly state the experimental question being investigated. The question should provide enough detail for the audience to understand what will be done in the experiment. (Example: "Which brand of raisin bran cereal is best in terms of flake size, quantity of raisins, and absorption of milk?")

Hypothesis: This should be a complete sentence, giving your hypothesis (an explanation, based on your observations, that can be tested by experiment). It is not a prediction (an educated guess), but it might be based on a prediction. Sometimes it helps to think of the hypothesis as an "if/then prediction."

Thinking About the Problem: This is one or two paragraphs long, giving brief background information on your chosen experimental topic. What is known about the topic? What remains unknown about the topic? How does your experiment fit into this context? Define and explain the major scientific concepts involved in your experiment. If applicable, state differences among various product brands, including cost and nutritional value (two topics that are not actual experiments, but examples of research).

Data Collection Materials: Create a complete list of all of the materials that you use. Some of them may make excellent props for use during your presentation.

Procedure Steps and Sketch: Draw and label a sketch that you can use to clearly describe the procedure steps. The steps (maximum of five listed and numbered steps) and sketch should enable you to explain what anyone else should do in order to replicate your same experiment. If you choose a Consumer Science experiment, you must conduct at least three different experiments on at least three different brands (cost and nutritional value comparisons do not count as "experiments" but do provide helpful information).

Variables: Make certain that you test and control all possible variables in your experiment. Remember: A good experiment tests only one independent variable at a time! Hold all other variables constant, while you are testing that one variable. Set up a control as a basis of comparison, so you can determine the actual changes in your experiment.

Results: At least one photo of your results must be included, unless you can bring in the actual results on presentation day. Bring in props, showing experimental materials used, as well. The results section of your poster should be organized into graphs, charts, tables, and/or day-by-day logs (these can be handwritten or drawn, if desired). Make sure that you label your graphs or charts, so the audience can understand them. Photos are preferred over actual results when the experiment involves chemicals, hazardous materials, plants, or animals. If you choose a consumer science experiment, you must include one bar graph, which shows cost comparisons per serving for each of your three product brands.

Presentation: You must describe the purpose and procedure for your experiment(s). Discuss how your variables were controlled. Discuss what you learned from background research on your topic ("Thinking About the Problem" section).

You must describe the types and quantities of data you collected. Discuss what you observed and what you measured.

You must compare your original hypothesis with your results. Look over your graphs, charts, tables, or daily log and then explain what you think the data show or seem to indicate. Include how your results are supported by other related scientific concepts, research, or theories (use your background research to help with this).

Finally, you must give one "I learned…" statement, and one "If I were to re-do this lab, I would change…" statement. Areas of future research could be described here, as well.

Props and Photos: Props are required. Along with the props and text portions of your presentation poster, you must include at least one photo, showing your final results, or you could bring in your actual final results.

Science Project Gallery Walk: During science class, on _____, we will set up our projects in the main office hallway. This will allow other students to learn from your findings as they walk through the hall. You will do a brief show and tell for others.

Table 6.5. Presentation Grading Rubric

General Poster Requirements:	
Correct spelling/grammar?	0 1 2
Word-processed text on poster?	0 1 2
Experiment Project Requirements:	
Title and category?	0 1
Problem statement?	0 1
Hypothesis?	0 1
Materials list?	0 1
Procedure steps and sketch?	0 1
Proper labels and titles on data?	0 1
Photo/props showing results?	0 1 2 3 4 5
Adequate experimental data?	0 1 2 3 4 5 6 7
Control of all variables?	0 1 2 3 4 5
Presentation Requirements:		
Description of purpose?	0 1 2	
Detailed experiment description?	0 1 2 3 4	
Overall outcome stated?	0 1 2	
"Thinking About The Problem" background info shared?	0 1 2 3 4 5 6	
Multiple-choice questions for audience?	0 1 2 3 4 5	
"If I were to re-do…" statement?	0 1 2	
"I learned…" Statement?	0 1 2	
On time?	Yes (Great!)	No (-10)

Teacher Comments:

Multiple-Choice Verbal Questions for the Audience: Your task is to create three challenging multiple-choice questions for use during your presentation. Students should be able to answer these questions after having been in the audience during your presentation. This educational technique has been shown to improve scores on standardized tests. What a lucky group of students you are!

Think through your Science Experiment Project. Develop three questions about main points covered by your results or background research.

The three questions, with multiple-choice options (a, b, c, and d), will be verbally posed to your audience at the end of your presentation.

There are four rules to follow in writing the answers to each of your multiple-choice questions:

(1) One wrong-answer choice should represent an attempt at humor.

(2) Only one answer choice can be right.

(3) You may not use "all of the above" or "none of the above."

(4) You must have a proofreader look at your questions in advance to make sure that they make sense and do not have complex issues that compromise their overall quality.

When presenting these multiple-choice questions to your audience after your project presentation, please read each question out loud. Students can then be called on to provide answers.

Sample Multiple-Choice Question Starters:

(1) The graph shows ___. According to the information, how many (how much) ___?

(2) What would happen if ___?

(3) What tool is used to find ___?

(4) If ___, then which will most likely occur?

(5) This experiment, shown in this picture, was probably set up to answer which of the following questions?

If You Do Not Know Where To Begin, Use The Following Procedures:

(1) Find a question you are curious about (you could search any number of "science fair ideas" sites on the internet or use one of the many ideas from class).

(2) Determine into which of the sciences the question fits (Earth, life, physical, or consumer).

(3) Do background research (search for related experiments, background information on the concepts, science theories, research, nutritional values and costs of brands, ingredients or construction materials for brands, and scientific concepts related to your topic) and write your "Thinking About the Problem" paragraphs.

(4) Form a hypothesis (an explanation based on your observations, which can be tested by experiment).

(5) Experiment and investigate, finding a way to answer your problem statement by manipulating and controlling variables (at least three experiments on at least three different brands, if you choose a consumer project).

(6) Compile all of the data and results (graphs, charts, tables, and day-by-day logs) and take photos of results, or be prepared to bring actual results for your presentation (a bar graph of cost-per-serving, if you choose a consumer project).

(7) Form a conclusion based on your results (answer the original question/ problem statement).

(8) Write three multiple-choice questions, with answers, for the audience.

(9) Prepare your poster, following the attached guidelines.

(10) Practice the presentation (use the attached rubric for help in this).

Possible Consumer Science Product Ideas: If you choose a consumer science experiment you must conduct at least three different experiments on at least three different brands (cost and nutritional value comparisons do not count as "experiments," but do provide helpful background research). Also, if you choose a consumer science experiment, you must include one bar graph, which shows a cost comparison per serving for each of your three product brands.

Only one student, per class hour, can choose a particular product. Topics will be assigned on a first-come-first-served basis. Ideas for products include but are not limited to:

(1)   Nonrechargeable batteries (Caution: may be expensive)

(2)   Diapers (control for similar size)

(3)   Paper towels (control for size differences)

(4) Laundry detergents (hand-washing only)

(5) Dishwashing detergents (hand-washing only)

(6) Laundry stain removers

(7) Carpet cleaners

(8) Window cleaners

(9) Bathtub cleaners

(10) Toothpastes or toothbrushes

(11) Kitchen sponges

(12) Hamburgers or french fries

(13) Chocolate-chip ice cream brands

(14) Grocery store produce (bananas, apples, pears, etc.)

(15) Markers

(16) Nonmicrowave-popped popcorn brands

(17) Toilet paper brands

(18) Face cloths

(19) Frozen pizzas (control for ingredients)

(20) Toenail polishes

(21) Band-Aids

(22) Flower quality (carnations, roses, etc.)

(23) School glues

(24) Packaging tape brands

(25) Crunchy cereals (control for ingredients—e.G., Varieties of raisin bran)

(26) Composition notebooks

(27) Chocolate-chip cookie recipes (control for ingredients)

(28) Sports balls (basketballs, tennis balls, etc.)

(29) Macaroni and cheese varieties

(30) Table napkins

(31) Interior or exterior paints

(32) Ballpoint pens

(33) Soccer shin guards

(34) Grocery store brown paper bags

(35) Disposable cameras

Science Project (Differentiation for Enriched)

A differentiated requirement, called the "Community Connection Assignment," can be added for additional learning opportunities. Though low in point value, it is important in terms of any social-justice issues related to your problem statement. To fulfill the requirements of this assignment, you must write a brief letter to the editor of the local newspaper, contact a local politician or organization, or attend/present at a community meeting related to your problem statement. Educate the public about an issue, inform the government about wise decisions they could make, advocate for new choices being made at a local community level. Look closely at your problem statement for society connections, and then find a way to act upon what you have learned. You must be able to submit proof of any community connection activities by _____.

Science Trivia

Scientists are basically problem-solvers who work to find the best possible answers to questions about nature. The questions that we have been working on in labs are answered by experiment. Some questions in science, however, are answered by research. Use encyclopedias, dictionaries, and other resources to find answers to each of the following questions. Along with the answer to each, you must write the word that you would look up if you were to verify your answer (write that word in the margin, next to each question).

(1) Name the eight classical planets in order of increasing distance from the Sun.

(2) What is the highest mountain in the world?

(3) What pigment makes leaves green?

(4) Which light, blue or red, has higher frequency?

(5) What are the seven states of matter (recent resource needed)?

(6) What are the three main parts of an atom?

(7) If your temperature is 37°C, do you have a fever?

(8) Would you be going farther if you went 10 miles or 10 kilometers?

(9) What is a meteorologist?

(10) What is the common name for the star Polaris?

(11) What does a botanist study?

(12) What is the chemical symbol and the atomic number for iron?

(13) What is believed to be created when a large star collapses?

(14) What is the largest living species of feline?

(15) During which era did dinosaurs rule the land?

(16) What two months contain an equinox?

(17) What are the three main fossil fuels?

(18) What galaxy are we in?

(19) What constellation represents a hunter with a sword and belt?

(20) What virus is believed to cause AIDS?

(21) Of the following, which was the largest dinosaur: Tyrannosaurus rex, seismosaurus, or apatosaurus?

(22) What comet can we see every 76 years (approximately)?

(23) What bird lays the largest egg?

(24) Name the five senses.

(25) What does a barometer measure?

(26) Of the following, which is the largest order of insect: coleoptera (beetles), diptera (flies), lepidoptera (butterflies/moths), or orthopetera (grasshoppers/crickets)?

(27) Which of the following machines did Johannes Gutenberg invent: ballpoint pen, printing press, or cotton gin.

(28) What do isobars represent?

(29) What is the only day of the week named for a planet?

(30) What are the four major blood groups?

(31) How many chambers are there in the human heart?

(32) What does DNA stand for? Where is DNA found?

(33) If you are increasing in latitude in the Northern Hemisphere, are you traveling east, west, north, or south?

(34) What is the common name for the constellation found within Ursa Major?

(35) Is a spider an insect?

(36) Every day, an average of 190 liters of blood are cleaned in which of the following: kidneys, lungs, or liver?

(37) What turns blue litmus paper red?

(38) What two things do bees collect?

(39) What part of the body does glaucoma strike?

(40) On whom would you use the Heimlich maneuver?

(41) What scale measures earthquakes? What machine generates this measurement?

(42) If you have a condition called "bromidrosis," do you have smelly breath, smelly perfume, or smelly armpits?

(43) How did pterodactyls get from one place to another? How long ago were they alive?

(44) What are the three major groups of rocks?

(45) What is the name of the point at which condensation begins?

(46) Which two months contain a solstice?

(47) What causes the Earth to have seasons?

(48) Would you find your philtrum under your nose, tongue, or chin?

(49) For what work in physics did Einstein receive his Nobel Prize?

(50) What does RADAR stand for?

(51) What does SCUBA stand for?

(52) What does LASER stand for?

(53) Name the seven groups used in the classification of living things, starting with kingdom.

(54) Why does Mars get more ultraviolet radiation from the Sun than the Earth does?

(55) What causes the phases of the Moon?

Answer the following five questions using your own opinions:

(56) If you could travel in time, when and where would you go, and why?

(57) If you could be any insect, what would you be, and why?

(58) If you could live anywhere, in what climate would you chose to live, and why?

(59) If you could be an omnivore, carnivore, herbivore, or scavenger, which would you chose, and why?

(60) If you could choose any science-related career and begin it immediately, what would the career be, and why?

The Poetry of Earth Science

Your task is to create four poems about each of the four Earth science topics we have covered this year (astronomy, geology, meteorology, and physical oceanography). The poems must be completely designed and written by you.

Why should you do a good job on this assignment? Writing poetry requires that you become a careful observer; all scientists must possess this skill. Writing poetry helps develop your ease with imaginative language, a precursor to the abstract thinking necessary for success in science. The combination of concept-learning and writing poetry helps you function as a problem-solver, rather than just an information receiver. And, perhaps most important, you will learn science better when you are required to compare and contrast, summarize, describe, and interpret—all are important facets of poetic writing.

Each of your four poems must have a title. You will work on your own to complete this assignment. You must be willing to share any two of your poems with the class. You must choose from any of the following poetry patterns:

"Tanka"

Tanka is a type of Japanese poetry that contains 5 lines and 31 syllables arranged in a 5-7-5-7-7 pattern.

Example:

I like all Weather

Let's go out and enjoy it

Forever changing

Hide from it on occasion

Nature's own video game.

"I used to be...but now I am..."

Use three to five sentence starters as a pattern to describe scientific concepts.

Example:

I used to be granite,

But now I am gneiss.

I used to be slate,

But now I am shale.

I used to be just sand,

But now I am sandstone.

"Diamante"

A diamante is a seven-line poem that compares opposites using specific parts of speech. The diamond shape of the finished product gives this poem its name.

Line 1: nouns for the subject

Line 2: two adjectives describing the subject

Line 3: three action terms

Line 4: four nouns, two about the subject, two about its antonym

Line 5: three action terms describing the antonym

Line 6: two adjectives describing the antonym

Line 7: the antonym

Example:

Sun

Hot and radiating

Powerful, energetic, and strong

Gases, gravity   Rock and Ice

Revolving, rotating, together for always

Colder and reflecting

Planets

"Alphabet Pyramid"

These are five-line cumulative poems that contain specific parts of speech that begin with the same letters.

Line 1: the letter

Line 2: a noun

Line 3: add an adjective

Line 4: add a verb

Line 5: add an adverb

Example:

C

Contrails

Continuous contrails

Continuous contrails circulate

Continuous contrails circulate convincingly

"Cinquain"

A cinquain is a five-line descriptive poem that contains about 22 syllables.

Line 1: the subject

Line 2: four syllables describing the subject

Line 3: six syllables showing action

Line 4: eight syllables expressing a feeling or observation about the subject

Line 5: two syllables renaming the subject

Example:

Earth

Rocky planet

Cycling, changing, and warm

Amazing, fragile, and vital

Our home

Oh, the Science-Related Places You Could Go. . . (A Family Homework Opportunity)

Your Task: You have one month, which includes our spring break week, to go to a science-related place with your family and learn as much as you possibly can. It can be, but it does not have to be, in our state/province. Answer the six questions, and turn in your completed form by _____.

Questions:

Specifically where did you go (full name and address)?

When did you go (must be between _____ and _____)?

Who went with you?

Brief description of the science-related aspects of the event/location:

Student responses to the following:

- I learned…

- I most enjoyed…

Parent(s) responses to the following:

- I learned…

- I most enjoyed…

- Parent/guardian signature _____

Posttest for Earth Science

Directions: Read each sentence carefully. Find the correct word that best completes each sentence from the alphabetized word bank. Write the number code next to that word in the space beside each sentence. Not all words from your word bank will be used.

Word Bank:

(1) air mass
(2) albedo
(3) asteroid
(4) astronomy
(5) atmosphere
(6) ballast
(7) barometer
(8) biology
(9) buoyancy
(10) calculations
(11) chemists
(12) chemistry
(13) clouds
(14) comet
(15) debris
(16) earth
(17) energy
(18) environments
(19) estimations
(20) floats
(21) forces
(22) galaxies
(23) geologic time scale
(24) geologists
(25) geology
(26) glaciers
(27) greater
(28) higher tides
(29) hot spots
(30) human

(31) hydrologic
(32) imprints
(33) inference
(34) landforms
(35) length
(36) less
(37) lower tides
(38) mass
(39) mathematically
(40) meteorology
(41) minerals
(42) observations
(43) oceanography
(44) phase change
(45) properties
(46) relative humidity
(47) resources
(48) rocks
(49) seismic
(50) silt
(51) sinks
(52) size
(53) technology
(54) temperatures
(55) terrestrial
(56) theoretically
(57) water
(58) water vapor
(59) weather
(60) weather maps

Statements:

(1) An ___ is your interpretation or explanation of what you observe.

(2) Very careful observers from many cultures were able to explain astronomical events ___, with reliability, predictability, and precision.

(3) The distances between the planets are immensely larger than the ___ of the planets themselves.

(4) Two of the most important process skills that scientists use every day are___ of measurement and manipulation of standard laboratory equipment.

(5) By comparing the Gas Giants and the ___ planets we can gain insight into the formation of our solar system.

(6) The fraction of the light falling on a solar system object that is then reflected back into space is called its "___."

(7) Differences between ___ on the Moon and on Earth affect your survival, and would make your life very different.

(8) A ___ is a leftover remnant of the early formation of the solar system, with a magnificent tail that can stretch halfway across the sky.

(9) The world's first artificial satellite, named Sputnik, was launched by the Soviet Union in 1957, and its job was to collect data on atmospheric ___.

(10) ___ are Earth materials that have four main characteristics: they are solid, inorganic, and naturally occurring, and they have a definite chemical structure.

(11) Scientists use various___ —such as hardness, luster, color, and specific gravity—to help identify minerals.

(12) There are three main groups of ___: igneous, sedimentary, and metamorphic.

(13) Through research and evidence, including the use of the ___, most scientists conclude that the Earth is approximately 4.6 billion years old.

(14) Within layers of rock are records of events that have occurred on Earth, including the remains and/or ___ of the different plants and animals that have lived on Earth.

(15) Soil textures are determined by the percentages of clay, ___, and sand that is found in the soil.

(16) An earthquake is the result of a sudden release of energy in the _____ crust that creates _____ waves.

(17) Volcanoes form where magma burns through the crust, at subduction zones, at spreading centers, or at "___" like Hawaii.

(18) The continuous movement of water in a cyclic pattern is called the ___ cycle.

(19) The instrument used to measure atmospheric pressure is called a ___ and it is essential in weather forecasting.

(20) A ___ refers to whether a substance like water is a solid (ice), liquid (water), or a gas (water vapor).

(21) ___ is a measure of how much water vapor is actually in the air compared with the amount the air could possibly hold.

(22) When a warm air mass meets a cool ___, two distinct bodies of air are brought in contact, each with its own temperature and relative humidity.

(23) When the air is cool, it cannot hold as much ___ as when the air is warm, and therefore, less water will evaporate.

(24) By including information from a number of different stations, ___ will give a good idea of what the weather is across the whole area represented.

(25) It is possible to predict short-term weather changes with some accuracy just by looking at the ___.

(26) Large amounts of ___ must be added to water to achieve even a relatively small change in temperature.

(27) Although ___ is the most abundant substance on Earth's surface, very little of it is pure hydrogen and oxygen.

(28) Since water is more easily moved than land, ocean water gets pulled over the land area that happens to be facing the Moon, causing the side of the Earth closest to the Moon to experience ___.

(29) ___ is actually a result of the water pushing upward on objects.

(30) When the amount of ___ is kept constant, careful observers can begin to notice other characteristics of floating objects that influence how low they sit in water.

(31) We know that buoyancy depends on two main things: the ___ of the object and the volume of water it displaces.

(32) For an object to float, its mass must be equal to or ___ than the volume of the water it displaces.

(33) A Depth Diver ___ when we squeeze the bottle because the displaced water compresses any air in it.

Teacher Notes for Statements

Below you will find the question numbers, in order, followed by the correct answers and, in parentheses, the numbers of those answers in the word bank.

(1) inference (#33)
(2) mathematically (#39)
(3) size (#52)
(4) estimations (#19)
(5) terrestrial (#55)
(6) albedo (#2)
(7) environments (#18)
(8) comet (#14)
(9) temperatures (#54)
(10) minerals (#41)
(11) properties (#45)
(12) rocks (#48)
(13) geologic time scale (#23)
(14) imprints (#32)
(15) silt (#50)
(16) seismic (#49)
(17) hot spots (#29)
(18) hydrologic (#31)
(19) barometer (#7)
(20) phase change (#44)
(21) relative humidity (#46)
(22) air mass (#1)
(23) water vapor (#58)
(24) weather maps (#60)
(25) clouds (#13)
(26) energy (#17)
(27) water (#57)
(28) higher tides (#28)
(29) buoyancy (#9)
(30) ballast (#6)
(31) mass (#38)
(32) less (#36)
(33) sinks (#51)

Appendix C: Student Assessment and Procedural Documents

Figure 6.3. Science Safety Rules

Science Safety Rules

The following list of safety procedures pertains to my safety in the science classroom:

Horseplay in the science classroom is dangerous. I will practice appropriate conduct in the classroom, such as: walking, using a quiet voice, keeping my hands off others, etc. I will keep my mind and eyes on what I am doing.

I will follow written and verbal instructions concerning procedures and/or precautions. They are created for my protection.

Experiments done in class are for instruction. They are planned to teach an idea or concept. I will perform only authorized experiments.

I will handle only those chemicals or equipment for which I have received instruction. I will be extremely careful with handling and storage of chemicals, equipment, and sharp objects.

Chemicals are labeled to identify them. I will always read the label to make sure I am using the correct substance. Mixing and handling chemicals or other substances can be dangerous. I will not do so unless instructed in a planned and approved experiment.

When working with fire, I will not reach across a flame or bring any unauthorized substances near flames. I will not burn objects. I will keep long hair away from fire. I will never leave a burner unattended.

Safety equipment is provided in the science classroom in case of an emergency. I know how and when to use this equipment. I know where the eyewash station, fire blanket, and extinguishers are located.

It is required by law to wear safety goggles for many laboratory situations. To prevent injury, I will wear my goggles as instructed by the teacher.

Broken glass is dangerous. If an accident occurs, I will report it immediately to the teacher.

I will be careful not to write in books, on tables, on lab counters, or on desks. I realize that this is a form of vandalism and I will be held responsible for my behavior.

I will clean up after myself and my lab team. A messy area contributes to accidents.

Cheating and/or plagiarism will result in failure of the assignment. All work turned in by my classmates and me must be completely our own.

I will work to stop any bullying going on around me. Bullying is bad news.

Please sign and return this form to the teacher.

Name_____   Class hour_____

I have read the science safety rules. I understand these rules have been created for my protection. I agree to follow them and do my part to help make my science classroom a safe place to learn.

Signature of student: _____Date_____

Signature of parent/guardian: _____Date_____

Illustration 6.3. Lab Notebook Front Cover Page

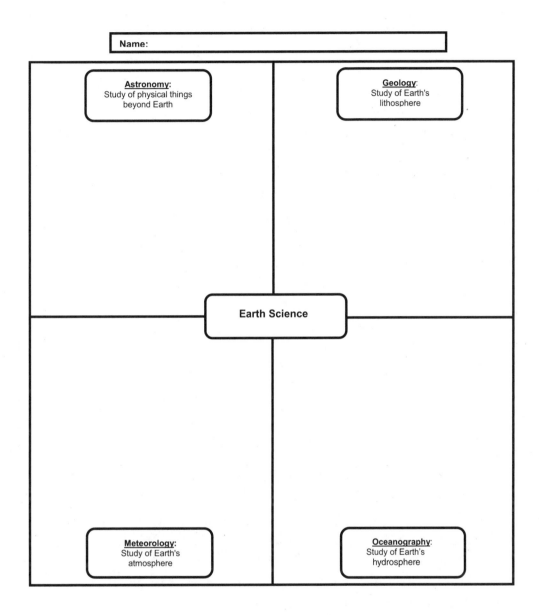

Name:

Astronomy:
Study of physical things
beyond Earth

Geology:
Study of Earth's
lithosphere

Earth Science

Meteorology:
Study of Earth's
atmosphere

Oceanography:
Study of Earth's
hydrosphere

Table 6.6. Lab Report Guidelines

Which sections must be in each Lab Report?

A. Anticipation Section Title—1 pt (written by students in the lab notebook)

B. Problem—1 pt (lab notebook)

C. Prediction—2 pts (lab notebook)

D. Thinking About the Problem—3 pts (handout, with main points in lab notebook)

E. Data Collection Materials (handout)

F. Data Collection Procedures—4 pts (steps in handout, labeled sketch in lab notebook)

G. Data Collection Tables—8 pts (lab notebook)

H. Analysis—6 pts (both questions and answers in lab notebook)

I. Concluding-the-Analysis Statements—5 pts (lab notebook)

J. Expansion and Further Investigation (optional; results turned in separately)

What are the Concluding-the-Analysis Statements mentioned above?

(1) "I Learned…" Statement (1 pt): These are facts and/or main ideas that apply to the lab you did. You must include the "I learned…" sentence starter.

(2) Re-do Statement (2 pts): Hypothesize a change in the variable(s) in an attempt to get a totally new outcome on the lab. An example might be: "I would try the experiment using a black light, rather than sunlight." A good sentence framework to use is "If I were to re-do this lab, I would change…"

(3) Identify a Variable and a Control (2 pts): A variable is an independent component of the experiment that is purposefully changed in order to see results. A control is a basis for comparison, and it remains unchanged during the lab. It allows you to determine what, if any, change took place in your variables during the experiment. A good sentence framework to use is "An example of a variable in this lab is…" and "An example of a control in this lab is…"

Note: What follows is a generalized grade. Please see the guidelines, above for the specific criteria used to grade each individual lab.

Table 6.7. Lab Notebook Grading Rubric

Aspect of Report	8	6	4	2
General appearance and organization	Lab notebook is neatly handwritten and fully complete. The Table of Contents and Grade Record Sheet are easy to follow. The notebook appears to be very well organized.	Lab notebook is relatively neat and mostly complete. The Table of Contents and Grade Record Sheet are a little hard to follow.	Many portions of the lab notebook are incomplete. The formatting does not help visually organize the material.	Lab notebook looks sloppy and/or is poorly organized. Most portions of the notebook are incomplete.

Student name: _____   Lab notebook score: ___/8

Extra credit opportunity (+1): My son/daughter has shown me the composition notebook for science class during the past week.

Signed _____

Figure 6.4 Self-Evaluation Tool

Self-Evaluation: To receive a good grade on your lab report, ask yourself the following 10 questions before submitting the report:

1. Is the anticipation section title complete and accurate? (1 pt)

2. Is the problem statement a complete sentence and phrased as a question? (1 pt)

3. Is my prediction a complete sentence and on-topic? (2 pts)

4. Do I have three complete sentences that give paraphrased, yet detailed, main points from the "Thinking About the Problem" section? (3 pts)

5. Did I draw a labeled sketch that shows the experiment procedure? (4 pts)

6. Is the information on my data collection tables and graphs complete and accurate? (8 pts)

7. Have I copied the analysis questions and answered them completely, with accuracy? (6 pts)

8. Do I have good "I learned…" and "re-do" statements, in complete sentences? (3 pts)

9. Do I have one variable and one control stated in complete sentences? (2 pts)

10. Were the sections required for my lab notebook completed on time? (subtract 7 pts from total score, if turned in late)

Index

*Page numbers in **boldface** type refer to tables or figures.*

Index